The Korean Center for Nonviolent Communication SM

Publisher:
The Korean Center for Nonviolent Communication
3F. Namyang BLDG. 23, Samseong-ro 95-gil,
Gangnam-gu, Seoul, South Korea

e-mail: krnvc@book.org

Graphic design:
Ivan Savić

Editor:
Nada Ignjatović Savić

Edition: fourth

Number of copies: 2000

Printed by:
South Korea

South Korea 2018.

Nada Ignjatović-Savić:

SMILE KEEPERS 2

Program for promoting self and social awareness development
psychological workshops for children 11-15 years of age

EDITION "SMILE KEEPERS 2", 2007

FOREWORD

Ten years have passed since the first edition of this manual, and we do have reasons for joy and celebration. Teachers highly appreciate Smile Keepers 2 program, hence they keep introducing new groups of children to it. Although the author no longer has an accurate count, we estimate that the program currently involves over one hundred thousand children.

2002 - The program was included in the Catalogue of Programs accredited by the Ministry of Education of Serbia and recommended for professional training of teachers.

2003-2004 - In cooperation with the educational program team of the national TV Channel the author initiated "Smile Keepers", a TV serial of 33 workshop episodes with the same group of children, widely welcomed by children audiences. This year the second showing of TV "Smile Keepers" will be aired by the educational program of the national TV network.

2006 - In cooperation the Methodic Center for Psycho-pedagogic Assistance in Education in Poland (MPPP), the author has trained a team of teacher trainers to conduct Smile Keepers programs with children in Poland. The programs are translated into Polish.

2006 - several groups of teachers from Germany, Switzerland, Belgium, France and Luxembourg expressed interest in applying for this program in their own schools. That would account for publishing this edition.

This edition is extended by one workshop aiming at informing children's parents about the program and its effects (32) , and 13 new workshops on the themes the teachers reported as important for the children (1, 11, 12, 13, 19, 20, 21, 22, 23, 24, 25, 26, 27) .

INTRODUCTION

"There are rivers in each of us
Meeting under this very same bridge,
That's why our happiness and sadness
Are so differently of the same kind."

Miroslav Antić
"This Is How I Imagine Heaven"

This manual is intended for professionals - psychologists, pedagogues, and teachers - working with children in the upper grades of elementary school. The program of psychological workshops for promoting self and social awareness development in children presented in this manual was concei-ved within a wider project, at the Institute of Psychology in 1993 under the name: Smile Keepers. The project sponsored by the UNICEF has been carried out since February 1993 in kindergartens and schools in Serbia and Montenegro.

The main goal of the psychological workshops program is to promote chil-dren personality development. Through interactions in a playful context they have opportunities:
- to develop self and social awareness,
- to become aware of their own uniqueness, mutual differences and similarities,
- to enrich their experiences and problem solving skills,
- to build their emotional stability,
- to develop optimal strategies to overcome unpleasant mental states or conflicts,
- to promote skills of self-expression and communication,
- to strengthen self-confidence as well as confidence in others,
- to acquire better understanding of their own selves and others.

Two other programs under the same name, i.e. "Smile Keepers 1" (containing activities for children 5-10), and "Smile Keepers 3"(for adolescents) have the same goal.
The "Smile Keepers 2" program was first introduced September through

December 1993 for about 3000 pupils (104 classes), in 33 elementary schools of the following cities: Arandjelovac, Bar, Beograd, Bijela, Budva, Gornji Milanovac, Kragujevac, Kotor, Leskovac, Loznica, Ljubovija, Pancevo, Valjevo, and Tivat. The workshops were lead by 211 teachers in the above-mentioned schools. On publishing the first edition in early 1997, the Smile Keepers Program had been conducted in more than 50 places, with more than 2000 adult "smile keepers" and over 21000 children participating in the program.

AN EVALUATION OF THE PROGRAM EFFECTS
A SHORT OVERVIEW

Three different types of data were collected, all of them testifying to the positive effects of the program on the children's behavior:

1. **Children's self-estimates of their benefits from the program** – children were asked if, and what kind of effects they attributed to the program. According to the observation of the majority of them significant changes occurred on 3 levels:
   a. **On a personal level**:
   - Their self-confidence and confidence in others increased
   - They acquired insight about their similarities and differences
   - Their openness in expressing themselves increased as tensions among themselves decreased
   - They acquired some special skills and "know how" in overcoming personal problems.

   Here are some children's comments to illustrate this point:
   "My stage fright is gone, and I used to have it!"
   "Now I know that even the most difficult problem has a solution!"
   "I now feel I am worth something!"
   "I never looked so deep into my own self or learned so much about me as in this program!"
   "Now I know that the other kids have fears, too!"
   b. **On a peer level** children consider there is more closeness and harmony between them.
   c. **Relationship with teachers:** They report how much they appreciated the chance to express their fears, anger, sadness in the presence of the teacher and have his/her support and understanding. They very much liked the non-directive approach of the workshop leader. "In the workshop I am free to be as I am, and the best of all is that no one is criticizing me for that!"
2. **Quantitative estimates of children's behavior done by workshop**

leaders - the workshop leaders assessed all children on behavior screening checklists before and after the program. The checklist consisted of 20 attributes of behavior, 10 formulated in positive terms, 10 in negative terms. The presence of each attribute in the behavior of the child was assessed on a 1-5 scale.

The differences between quantitative estimates made for each child for all attributes before and after the program were analyzed in order to identify individual progress. T–test was done to check if the differences were accidental or statistically significant and could be seen as effects of the program. Results show significant progress in the expected direction, i.e. significant increase in positive in conjunction with decrease in negative attributes. In other words, children who took the program become more open minded, felt free to express their feelings, grew more sensitive, determined, sociable, imaginative, curious and independent. On the other hand they became less fearful, tense and passive.

3. **Qualitative estimates of the effects of the program done by workshop leaders** - in their reports the workshop leaders pointed out the following changes observed in the behavior of children:

Children became more joyful, tolerant, and open in communication, more expressive in sharing their feelings, more willing to acquire insight of themselves and others, to look for motives and feelings behind certain acts.

Workshop leaders also noticed the improvement in the overall classroom atmosphere: there was less aggressiveness as more cooperation occurred both among children and in their relationship with teachers.

Workshop leaders pointed out that the program helped them get to know all children better. They were especially satisfied seeing the positive effects of the program on introverted children who were able to manifest abilities and features they had not known or wanted to show before.

In this short overview of the results of evaluation we focused on presenting only the most conspicuous data. The image about positive effects is actually much richer.

That is why the main reason for publishing this manual resides in our wish to make it available to a larger number of teachers who intend to support development of the personality of children they work with.

Still, the author's dilemma stays: will somebody who has had neither the training nor the direct personal experience with this kind of workshops ever be able to use this manual adequately and create quality of contact, a distinctive feature of Smile Keepers program.

TRAINING OF THE WORKSHOP LEADERS

Before starting to work with children, all workshop leaders had to attend 16 workshops i.e. a 32-hour special training program. The purpose of the training was to give them the chance to learn about the content and goal of each workshop and acquire the skills of leading a workshop by themselves through direct experience and active development of their own expertise in the field. Moreover, the training aimed at enhancing their pedagogical competence by practicing alternative, rather than traditional patterns in education.

Namely, when children express negative emotions the usual adults' reactions are: diverting child's attention to something else (when sad), persuading the child (when afraid), forbidding and punishing the child (when angry). In our cultural context, it is very rare that adults would offer what the child overwhelmed by fear, anger or sadness desperately needs – an empathic response such as: "Are you sad because you would like to be at home, with those close to you?" "Are you angry because you wanted respect for your proposal?"

The adult's emphatic reaction would be beneficial in many ways: it strengthens mutual confidence and closeness because the child is realizing that his feelings are acknowledged, it enables further exchange and gives the child a chance to become aware of the connection between his feelings and needs, as well as realize more clearly how the adult could help him in overcoming unpleasant situations. It is very often that all the child needs is just to be heard by the adult, as he is not asking for help or advice in solving his problems.

In a research study carried out in Belgrade in 1992, we asked kindergarten and school teachers to write down how they would react in three different situations: when the child tells them about his/her conflict with peers, when the child refuses to do what he/she was asked to do, and when the child acts angrily because he/she is feeling hurt.

None of the180 teachers ever gave an emphatic answer (see table 1 and table 2, page 6).

The most frequent adult reactions:
- to children sharing about their conflicts with peers was giving advice,
- to children refusing to obey was offering a logical explanation,
- to children with emotional outbursts was denying feelings.

The alarming fact is that a more intense emotion (as in the third situation) will trigger a more frequent adult denial.

Moreover, one could notice inconsistencies between educational goals and practical, concrete steps teachers used to reach these goals. When asked about the most significant educational goals with children, the overwhelming majority of teachers mentioned independence and responsibility.

table 1. Schoolteachers – categories of reactions to the 3 different situations

	Reaction of the adult	Child's conflict with peers (f)	(%)	Child's disobedience (f)	(%)	Child's emotional outburst (f)	(%)
1	demanding	0	0	3	3	6	7
2	threatening	0	0	3	3	6	7
3	moralizing	9	10	24	27	14	15
4	giving advice	54	60	24	27	10	11
5	Offering a logical explanation	15	17	27	30	0	0
6	criticizing	0	0	3	3	0	0
7	expressing agreement	0	0	0	0	3	3
8	interpreting	6	7	0	0	6	7
9	sympathizing	3	3	2	2	0	0
10	inquiring	3	3	0	0	6	7
11	denying feelings	0	0	4	5	39	43
		90	100	90	100	90	100

table 2. Preschool teachers - categories of reactions to the 3 different situations

	Reaction of the adult	Child's conflict with peers (f)	(%)	Child's disobedience (f)	(%)	Child's emotional outburst (f)	(%)
1	demanding	3	3	9	10	18	20
2	threatening	0	0	3	3	0	0
3	moralizing	3	3	15	17	0	0
4	giving advice	36	40	0	0	3	3
5	offering a logical explanation	0	0	45	50	3	3
6	criticizing	15	17	3	3	6	7
7	expressing agreement	0	0	0	0	6	7
8	interpreting	12	14	0	0	18	20
9	sympathizing	0	0	0	0	0	0
10	inquiring	18	20	3	3	0	0
11	denying feelings	3	3	12	14	36	40
		90	100	90	100	90	100

Yet, when asked about the concrete steps towards promoting these be-havioral features, very few of them mentioned offering opportunities to chil-dren for making their own decisions or freely expressing their needs. "I want the child to be responsible" and "I promote this by insisting that he finish his homework first, and then go and play" can hardly be considered encouraging either independence or responsibility. By taking responsibility for what the child should plan or do, the adult is actually suppressing child's autonomy.

The way adults reacted was in discord with their own intended goals which actually were to support, promote, and develop child's independence as well as other desired personality traits. Paradoxically, their way of caring out their intentions was inducing quite opposite effects. Even more paradoxical is that in most of the cases the adults were aware of it! What they didn't know was the adequate way to react.

That was the reason why we considered that our main task in designing the adults' education program was to offer them the "know-how". We selected those kind of training activities which, on the one hand will give adults the chance to reflect on their educational practices, to elaborate the goals they want to achieve, to design the steps as well as consider the consequences of their educational interventions, and on the other to make them acquire experience and practice, ways and means more adequate to their goal - to support children in becoming more independent, responsible, and creative by respecting both themselves and the others.

Whoever tries to put this program of workshops with children into practice without previous training is very likely to miss this experience or the "know-how" about acting and reacting towards developing and stimulating in the children the desired behavioral traits.

Anyway, those who are planning to put this program of workshops into practice should have knowledge of psychological characteristics of children 11-15 years of age, and the ability to:

- listen with empathy, neither judge or rush into verdicts, analyses, criticism, or patronize;
- enjoy playful atmosphere;
- carry out open-minded exchange and "expect the unexpected";
- tune their intervention towards stimulating and motivating children rather than giving instructions.

The most important task in children education is to support them build a positive image about themselves, develop their self-confidence and independence, make them have personally enriching experiences by giving to and receiving from the others.

THEORETICAL BACKGROUND

The theoretic basis of this program is a combination of interactivist and constructivist approach to the nature of human development, relying on Vygotskian's theory of development and M. B. Rosenberg's Model of Nonviolent Communication.

The following theses are relevant for the program:

The adults mediate a child's experience of the world and himself in that world.

We consider it an optimal situation when adults:

- organize environment and sharing in such a way that children can understand and accept it;
- help the children to face relevant, specifically chosen stimuli which lead them to higher stages of development and protect them from experiences hard to cope with at this age;
- encourage every spontaneous attempt a child makes to explore and learn about himself and the world and try to make it a pleasant, positive experience for the children.

Intervention in the zone of proximal development is a decisive factor of the developmental change. The main task of anyone trying to foster mental development of children is to support those mental processes that are "in embryonic state" with children, but could be facilitated by mutual interaction between the adult and the child.

Adults play a delicate role in discerning promoting development from direct intervention. The magic key for any hesitation on how to intervene is a compassionate approach in the form of an empathic question: "Do you now feel ...because you need?"

Interested readers can find more detailed information about the process of compassionate approach in M. B. Rosenberg's books on his model of nonviolent communication (visit www.cnvc.org).

Children are active participants in the interaction.

- It is the child who initiates, chooses, re-arranges, and keeps for him-self just elements in concord with his developmental needs and ca-pacities;
- the path from outer to inner space, from exchange to creating an inner, private, psychological world goes through independent, individual symbolic activities by which a child in his/her special way puts together things collected through a wide range of exchanges.

Child development is not only about changes in mental functions but

also about changes in the mutual relationships among them, i.e. in their organization.

- Beside changes within each mental function developmental change consists in changing mutual relationships between these functions, in changing the place and role of a particular mental function in the system of mental organization.
- A crucial role in potentially different patterns of integration of mental functions is given to the meta-cognition, i.e. the self-reflection and deliberate control of the way mental functions work.
- The origin of meta-cognition is in social interaction. Symbolic play has an important role in the process of internalization (transformation of inter-psychic to intra-psychic). The context of play gives greater degrees of freedom and activates different layers of the child's interior world, providing for more chances for a new pattern to emerge.

BASIC PRINCIPLES OF THE APPROACH

- There is no authority - all participants are equal, meaning that the workshop leader as well as the assistant participate and share their personal experiences too.

- Adults organize activities in such a way that children get a need and desire to share **among themselves and not only with adults**.

- Adults create an **atmosphere of confidence and acceptance** by avoiding to pass judgments, criticism, interpretation, or to give advice or direct suggestions of the solution. It is important for children to feel comfortable and relaxed.

- The accent is on the **process** of discovery and learning, not on the outcome.

- The workshop leader applies an indirect, **lateral approach**. The paradox of change is that if forced to change, one conserves oneself. Hence it is necessary to offer a new context, an unusual point of view and let everybody put the pieces together in their own way, create conditions for the change and not force it.

- It is important that learning is achieved through **playing**, not through lecturing.

- There are **no ready-made solutions**, right answers for the child to remember – the adult is not a person who asks questions already knowing the answer he wants to get from the children. The adult is nurturing an attitude of "expecting the unexpected", because developmental change is by definition something new.

• The adult should be able to give right and well-timed stimulation to each child, he needs to know how to listen with special attention and sensitivity and how to be open to consider and give importance to what children communicate. The poet Duško Radović through his "**respected children**" gave the shortest and most articulate approach of the kind.

• The adults **stimulate** (**working in zone of proximal development**) without forcing anything on children, they flexibly move between symmetric and asymmetric positions, between support and stimulation.

• The adults nurture a **positive** approach and encourage children to enjoy their own acquisitions, to feel and express satisfaction with themselves by making **concrete** comments ("I like that you did it that way") and not general ones ("You are good").

• The adults **respect resistance**: there is no *should*, if somebody does not want to take part in some activity.

• If **outbursts of negative feelings happen**, the adult gives time to children to come out of crying or anger without interrupting questions or stifling them. Empathic listening and questioning help the child make the difference between what he/she is feeling and why, that need is not met: "Are you sad because you want understanding?" "Are you angry because you want to choose what you want to do?"

• The adults give support and encouragement to the children to make them use their energy constructively and not hurt themselves or others.

• The adult intervention in the zone of proximal development is double-fold:

  1. **Indirect**: through the choice and structuring of the activities; coordinating a workshop as well as the program as a whole is intended to provide developmental, productive exchanges.

  2. **Direct** by:

    a. Giving a proper hint at proper time to evoke an individual child's insight.

    b. Monitoring the exchanges among children as a group in such a way as to help them benefit from mutual feedback. The variety of available models in a group may serve different age needs.

    c. Expressing his own meta-cognitive strategies and insights, whenever possible. The main point is to give a possible model, not to try shaping the behavior of children.

However, it is difficult to explicitly define what an intervention in the zone of proximal development is. Every workshop is an open system and its quality and level is changed in accordance with what participants bring into it. Sometimes the fact that the adult simply repeats what the child says is enough for the child to make progress, to have an insight. Sometimes, it is about making explicit a strategy someone else uses in a similar situation – in this case it is a trigger for the child to discover his own optimal strategy for addressing his own personal challenges.

WHAT IS IMPORTANT
for workshop leaders to know

• The optimal number of children-participants is from 10-15. You can work with the group up to 20 children, but then attention and motivation to share decreases. If the group is bigger, it is better to break it into two groups within which more intensive and better sharing could take place as every child has the chance to express himself and listen to the others. Subgroups should stay the same till the end of the program.

• This program of psychological workshops is designed for children aged 11 to 15.

• If possible, there should be two persons leading the workshops:
  - the **workshop-leader** who follows the script and stimulates the exchanges in the group;
  - the **assistant** who takes notes of everything children say and their performance from the first to the closing circle.
    The written report should contain the following data:
      - time, place, participants
      - name of the leader
      - all the activities that were carried out and their order as well as
      - all the responses of the children

• The optimal rhythm of work is of 1-2 workshops a week. In this way the workshop leader has enough time to decant impressions on every child and the children can work on the experience they had shared in the group through spontaneous symbolic activities.

• It is planned that every workshop lasts about an hour. Of course, it depends on the number of participants and on the level of their involvement in activities.

• Changes in scripts must be made according to the children's response, as the basic principle of the program is that adults adjust themselves to the children. Nevertheless, one should be aware of the fact that neither the sequence of workshops nor the activities within the workshop are occasional.

Each of these workshops respects the pattern: the activity that introduces the problem analysis (conflict, unpleasant emotional state, etc.), followed by the activity through which a child can find a constructive way out. Therefore, whatever the reason, the workshop should not be finished before children were given a possibility to learn how to overcome the things that bother them. At the same time, workshops should be organized so that children can gradually face unpleasant and painful topics but in closing workshops the focus is on positive feelings and active approach.

• **At the core of the program** there are activities requiring symbolic expression (drawing, pantomime, symbolic play, drama play) and sharing around the circle. Thus the children are able to develop awareness of their inner experiences. It is important to give enough time for every child to present and comment on his drawing.

• Relaxing exercise and games, gestures and movement help children release tension and generate good mood in the group. Therefore the workshop leader could introduce them whenever he feels the children are tired.

SPECIAL NOTES

NOTE: It could be a problem that children want to know how "good" they are in certain activities and try to guess what adults expect from them. It should be pointed out that they are expected to share what they genuinely feel and think.

NOTE: resistance is to be respected but when and who refuses to share something should be kept track of. Special attention should be paid to reserved (silent) children, i.e. encourage them but do not insist on involving them.

NOTE: If there are children who often interrupt and disturb group work, they should be kindly reminded of the rule by a gentle: "That is interesting, but wait for your turn to come!" If that doesn't help, try to make one comment on **how we feel when somebody interrupts** and the other one on **reasons that make us sometimes not to listen to others**.

NOTE: If the group refuses to work try to see what the problem is, adjust the script, play some games that the children are interested in.

WHAT TO TELL PARTICIPANTS
at the beginning of the program

- The essence of the program is that we are the "guards of the smile".

In short, the goal is:
- To learn something new about themselves and others;
- To learn to better understand and respect themselves and others;
- To discover how to resolve problems that bother them;
- To take delight in friendship;
- To learn some new games.

- They will have the chance to deal with serious matters in an amusing way, through play; there will be some drawing, pantomime, or writing on pieces of paper...

- There will be the chance to explore some new skills that they could later use alone, or in the circle of their friends (relaxation techniques, role playing, imagination exercises, etc.).

WHAT IS IMPORTANT FOR PARTICIPANTS IN THE WORKSHOP
to know in advance

- Sharing goes around the circle. The circle is thought to be the most democratic arrangement for no one can dominate and everybody has the same amount of space around him. It is very important that everyone can see and hear the others.

- Everybody takes active part - you talk when it is your turn and follow carefully what the others share, because that is a way for you to learn, too.

- If you do not want to participate in an activity, just say: "Pass!"

- Everybody contributes something personal but only as much as he/she wants.

- There are no expected/right answers; it is important that you share something you feel or think.

There are some **rules** we need to agree on and respect from the very beginning:

- Respect the rule of confidentiality: what is shared within the circle should not leave the circle, no gossiping!

- There will be fun and laughing but not ridiculing.
- Mutual listening and tolerance for differences are important elements of interaction. The point is that everyone is unique and special and our differences could enrich us.
- No new members are accepted after the program has started.
- There are no observers, everybody who is present participates.
- Come in time.
- Do not go out during the workshop (it would disturb everybody).
- Come to the workshops regularly. The workshops are interrelated and there is order in topics to make progress gradual toward more complex topics. That's why it is important to attend the workshops regularly and not miss a single one. There will be 31 workshops on different topics, one or two per week.
- The class will be divided into two groups that do the same things, because it is important that everyone has a chance to participate actively… (if this is a case).
- After presenting the program, give participants a chance to ask questions about what they are interested to know about the program, and to say what they expect from the workshops.

WORKSHOP No. 1

INTRODUCING THE PROGRAM AND THE METHODOLOGY OF WORK

THE WORKSHOP SCHEMA

1. Workshop leader presents the **content and the methodology** of work to the students

2. The **game of not listening** in a large group

3. **Game of listening** in pairs

4. The **right to express** your own opinion

5. **Respect other's opinion**, do not discard it only because it is different from yours, try to understand the reasons for it, check your own thinking

6. **Right to privacy**

7. **Closing game**

INTRODUCING THE PROGRAM AND THE METHODOLOGY OF WORK

1. Workshop leader presents the **content and the methodology** of work to the students.
   See **What to tell participants at the beginning of the program**.
   - WL gives a short overview of all topics of the program.
   - WL gives a chance to children to ask about what they want to know.
   - WL reminds them: **What is important for participants to know about the workshops in advance.** Workshop rules that need to be respected (see the text about it in the introduction).

   WL points out that listening to one another is very important.
   WL invites children to play a game in which they will not listen to one another and experience what the class would look like.

2. The **game of not listening** in a large group
   WL asks the children to remember what they did last weekend and then, on his sign, asks all of them to start speaking about it at the same time.
   Sharing around the circle: How did they feel when they were talking without being listened to? Was it difficult to talk? Did they hear what the others were talking about?

3. **Game of listening** in pairs
   WL informs the children that they are now going to play the game of listening. WL points out that the task of the listener is to repeat everything that has been said, and that is why it is important to listen very attentively and to remember whatever was said. Children are organized into pairs, and decide who is no.1 and no.2 in the pair. When WL gives a sign, child no.1 starts to talk about his/her experiences during last weekend as child no.2 listens carefully, and when WL gives the STOP sign, reports on what has just

been said. After 1 minute WL says STOP. Child no.2 reports back on what has been said. Children switch roles, no.2 talking and no.1 listening and reporting.

Sharing with the group: Was it easy to talk? Was it difficult to listen? Did they succeed in reporting everything?

WL comments on how important it is for all of us to be listened to and how making a contribution gives us a pleasant feeling, develops friendship and makes us learn something new.

4. **The right to express your own opinion**

   WL informs the children that they have the right to express what they think even if it is dissonant with the opinions of the others, that every opinion is valuable, that it is important to stick to your opinion and make it clear to the others.

   WL draws two lines of equal length on the board, one below the other, but a little bit displaced to the right. Then he says: *You can see here two lines. I think the line below is longer than the one above. What do you think?*

   _____

     _____

   If the children agree, the WL reminds them how important it is to check before they agree, and in this case they can measure the length of both lines, and then decide if it is the same or different. If they do not agree, the WL asks them about their reason to think that way, and points out that checking can help the WL to change his opinion, too.

5. **Respect other's opinion**, do not discard it only because it is different from yours, try to understand the reasons for it, check your own thinking.

   WL writes big number 6 on an A4 paper and then sets it on the floor. He invites two students to stand next to it so that one is seeing number 6 and the other number 9. WL asks the two children about what they see. Then the WL asks the group which of the two is right.

   Sharing in the group: *Who is right? Why do you think so?*

   WL comments that the two students can quarrel about it or they can choose to put themselves into the skin of the other and understand each other's position. That way both of them will learn something new and there is no fight. When you do not agree with what the other says, take care not to say things that can hurt, but ask questions that will help you understand the other's way of thinking, and express reasons why you do not agree with it.

6. **Right to privacy**: WL reminds children to respect privacy, not to gossip after the workshop because that can hurt someone and disturb the atmosphere of friendship.

7. **Closing game**: WL invites children to teach him and others some circle game they know or like.

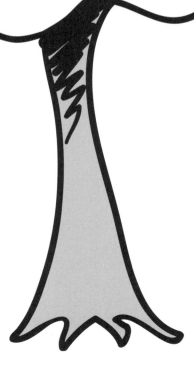

WORKSHOP No. 2

KNOW YOURSELF (SELF IDENTITY)

THE WORKSHOP SHEMA

1. **Getting to know each other**

2. **Transformation game**: *If you were an animal, what animal would you like to be?*

3. *What is making you unique*, special?

4. **Make your own badge**

5. **Take your badge for a walk**

THE GOAL of the workshop:
- to make children aware of themselves, their specific traits, the differences and similarities between them,
- to stimulate imagination,
- to encourage sharing.

KNOW YOURSELF (SELF IDENTITY)

1. **Getting to know each other**
   Say your name (the way you would like to be called here) and something you like to do ("My name is X and I like to...").
   The one sitting next to you in the circle is to repeat your statement adding to it his/her own statement ("X likes to..., and my name is Y and I like to...").

2. **Transformation game**: *If you were an animal, what animal would you like to be?* Give them a break to think about it. *Why? What is it that you like about that animal?* Short break followed by sharing around the circle: "I would like to be a.... because..."

3. ***What is making you unique**, special? What is it that you know or have?*
   Sharing around the circle: What makes them unique?

4. **Make your own badge**: it should contain your name and something typical for you - your personal sign, drawing or symbol of your choice (encourage them to use colors and the available material in their own way, to find their own shape, size, colors, their own language....
   Sharing around the circle: present and explain what is on the badge you made.

5. **Take your badge for a walk**: go around and introduce yourself to everyone in the group, see the other badges (prepare in advance something to fix the badges on the cloth) and say what you like about them.

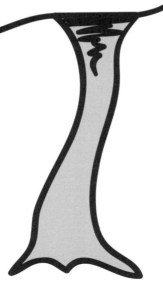

WORKSHOP No. 3

**LET'S LOVE OURSELVES
(PERSONAL IDENTITY)**

THE WORKSHOP SHEMA

1. **Circle of names**

2. **Think positively about yourself**

3. **The journey of discovery**

4. **Showing off walk**

5. **Negatively about yourself:** What was it that you did
   not like about yourself?

6. **Transformation game**

7. **Positive message to your neighbor:** Lets treat ourselves!

THE GOAL of the workshop:
- to stimulate positive attitude towards ourselves.

LET'S LOVE OURSELVES (PERSONAL IDENTITY)

1. **Circle of names:** *Call your own name gently by saying it tenderly.*

2. **Think positively about yourself:** *Think about three characteristics you would point out as the most valuable in you. Write them on a small piece of paper, and adorn them with drawings as if you were advertising.*

3. **The journey of discovery:** *Hide that piece of paper somewhere on you so that none of the others can see it (under your hair, collar etc.). You can shortly go out of the classroom to hide it.*
   When everybody has finished hiding their papers tell the children that they should walk around and try to discover as many of the others' papers as possible, and keep their paper hidden. The one who finds any of the papers is supposed to smile to its owner and say: "Oh, you are...." and than read aloud what is written on the paper. They should accompany this with: "Congratulations!" or "Nice to meet you!" or anything of the kind showing celebration at what was written.

4. **Showing off walk:** *Put that piece of paper somewhere on you again, this time in a highly visible place, show off as you walk proudly and display it for everybody to see.*
   Sharing around the circle: *What was easier for you, when you were hiding or showing off your characteristics?*
   What did you like in this game? What was it that you didn't like?

5. **Negatively about yourself:** *What was it that you did not like about yourself? Write one of yours characteristics you don't like on the paper?*
   Sharing around the circle: *What is it that you do not like about yourself?*

6. **Transformation game:** *Now let's see how we can change what we do not like into something we like. How you could change what you wrote or look differently, positively on it?*

Sharing around the circle: What did they do with things they did not like about themselves?

Workshop leader (WL) comment: *sometimes we find it difficult to show things about us to the others. Parents and teachers also tend to mostly comment on what they do not like about the children, whereas whatever they like they do not mention, inferring that children know it. The fact is that expressing positive things about us and the others is as important as food. It is like "charging our batteries"!*

7. **Positive message to your neighbor:** Let's treat ourselves!
   Send one positive message to your neighbor on the left side. Tell him/her what you like about him/her (the messages are going in a circle, with each and every child speaking in their turn).

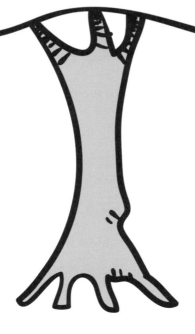

WORKSHOP No. 4

**IDEAL PLACE OF RELAXATION
(RELAXATION TECHNIQUE)**

THE WORKSHOP SCHEMA

1. **Circle of names**

2. **Quickening circle**

3. **Slowing down circle**

4. **The ideal place for relaxation**
   (demonstration of the relaxation technique).

5. Try to **make a drawing of your place of relaxation,** the best you can

6. **Confidence exercise in pairs: see - saw**

THE GOAL of the workshop:
- to bring to mind pleasant memories;
- to teach children how to relax;
- to stimulate imagination.

IDEAL PLACE OF RELAXATION (RELAXATION TECHNIQUE)

1. **Circle of names:** one is saying his name in a low voice, the other loudly, next one again in a low voice, etc.

2. **Quickening circle:** WL starts saying his name slowly, the child next to him speaks a little bit quicker, the next one quicker and so on. By the end of the circle the rhythm should be really fast.

3. **Slowing down circle:** it starts in fast rhythm and slows down towards the end of the circle.

4. **The ideal place for relaxation** (demonstration of the relaxation technique). Before the exercise, explain in few words that:
   - the children are off to an inner (mental) journey;
   - the children will do a relaxation and imagination exercise;
   - they should close there eyes but not force themselves into bringing images to their mind, they should let them come freely;
   - they should be quiet and attentive so that they can experience something beautiful;
   - if their thoughts start to wander, they are to follow them to see where they lead them, and then continue with the exercise;
   - if anything happens that they do not enjoy, they should have in mind that they can always open their eyes and take control of the situation that way.

This is to be said slowly, with a lot of pauses, giving children time to internalize the things you say:
RELAXING:
1. *Sit comfortably, with your feet on the floor, relaxed... relax your arms, palms on your knees... find a comfortable position for your head... relax your shoulders. Take your time... easy... try to find the most comfortable position...*

27

2. Look straight ahead and then lift your eyes half way ...just your eyes, not your head... focus on one spot and when you feel your eyes are tired, close them.

3. After 15 seconds the WP says: Close your eyes... try to breathe evenly... breathe in as you count to three... breathe out as you count to three. Imagine that your breathing calms you down as if you breathe out all the troubles... say to yourself: "Relax!"

4. Feel that you are here and now. We are in this room. Let yourself hear all the sounds, first the close and then the remote ones. (2 sec.) Sounds together are a halo giving you shelter, and you absorb into that halo every new sound you hear. No sound can disturb you. (2 sec.) You can hear, then name the strongest sounds, especially when some sudden sound occurs, and becomes part of the whole surrounding and protecting you.

5. Feel the wave of relaxation flowing down, from the top of your head, like a spiral, enveloping you and making you calm. Relax! (5 sec.)

6. Feel how that relaxing wave spreads. Feel the tension vanishing slowly, feel how your whole body relaxes: the head, eyelids, face, neck, shoulders, chest, back, arms, hands, belly, bottom, legs, feet, toes. The wave envelops you completely and makes you feel relaxed.

(5 sec. pause, then):

GUIDED FANTASY

1. Now, protected in this way, we are going on a journey. My voice will lead you, and you will imagine what you wish and what you enjoy most. If my words disturb you, just follow your own stream.

2. Imagine that you are somewhere out in the country. Move slowly across the soft, warm ground. Choose your own way of moving - you can walk, roll, float. Hear the sounds, first the close ones, then those from the distance. This could be the sound of the wind, or rain, birds singing, water... feel the colors and the light. The colors are pleasant and they make you feel relaxed. You move on and feel a light breeze touch your face, arms and body as if caressing you. Then sense other kinds of touch. It could be raindrops, snow, the sun... things you like. Relax! Now let yourself feel the scents: the scent of the ground, the scent of the plants. Breathe them in slowly and deeply, and relax. You are still moving on, easy relaxed, feeling all these pleasant sensations around you. (5 second break). Protected and relaxed in this way, you approach your place for relaxation. Everything that makes you feel calm and satisfied is going to be there the moment you wish it. You can slowly begin creating your ideal place of relaxation. (10 second break). Add to it everything you like. (5-6 second break). Make yourself comfortable, look around... let yourself sense the colors... light... shapes... sounds... touches... scents... (break). They are here... all around you... like a halo... to protect you. (5 second break).

Now you can slowly prepare to come back. Start slowly. When you feel like it, open your eyes and you are again in the classroom. Open your eyes! If you want to stand up and stretch your arms and legs, feel free to do so.

5. ***Try to make a drawing of your place of relaxation**, the best you can. Using lines, shapes and colors, express: where you were, how you felt, what you saw and experienced. It does not matter how you draw, what's important is that it means something to you. Find your own symbols... then, give a title to your drawing and write it down on it (the title should express your experience as briefly as possible).* **Sharing around the circle:** *What is your ideal place of relaxation? Where were you? How did you feel? When were you relaxed the most? What made you feel that way? What is the title of your drawing and why?*

6. **Confidence exercise in pairs: see - saw**. Children stand in pairs holding each other by the wrists as they squat and stand up together, simultaneously. They do it a couple of times. (Go around and help if necessary).

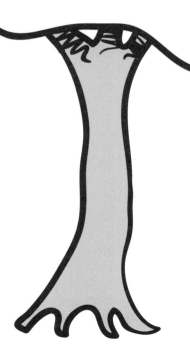

WORKSHOP No. 5

TIME TRAVEL (SELF-CONTINUITY)

THE WORKSHOP SCHEMA

1. **Names circle:** say your name in reverse

2. **Give a title to this day**

3. **Time travel**

4. **Pleasant memories**

5. **Confidence exercise**

THE GOAL of the workshop:
- to make children aware of their own development, the differences and similarities they share;
- to see what the important (pleasant and unpleasant) points in life are;
- to make pleasant memories active;
- to stimulate positive feelings and positive attitude towards oneself and others.

TIME TRAVEL (SELF-CONTINUITY)

1. **Names circle:** say your name in reverse (Marko - Okram).

2. **Give a title to this day:** *close your eyes and try to review this day, from the moment of waking up till now, as if it were a movie. Remember where you went, what you did, what you experienced, how you felt. Open your eyes. If this day were a script for a movie, what would be the name of the movie? Use your own name in the title, for example "Alice in Wonderland"* (Encourage them to say the first thing that comes to their mind, not to think too much.)
   Sharing around the circle: *Let's hear those titles! Why did you choose that title?*

3. **Time travel**
   Now we shall travel far into the past. We enter the time machine. Close your eyes and sail towards your childhood. Try to get to the beginning. (Short break) *Pay attention to:*
   - *how you move: in one way, skipping details, gradually;*
   - *where you stop* (pause);
   - *at which periods of your life do you think you were changing, when not* (pause).

   Open your eyes. Imagine your journey as a line. How would it look like? Draw your life line: choose your own shape, colors, symbols the way that suits you the best (pause), *mark in your own way the places on the drawing you think are important.* (pause) *Using your own symbols again, mark all the places where you felt good. Using different symbols mark the unpleasant, painful spots. If the drawing were a movie script, what title would it have? Write it down on your drawing.*
   Sharing around the circle: everybody shows his/her drawing, says the title and explains it in few words.

WL COMMENT: *It happens sometimes to all of us that unpleasant moments overshadow the pleasant ones, that they color our past, even our future. Nevertheless we get our energy out of pleasant experiences. That is why an effort of will is needed*:

4. **Pleasant memories:** *Concentrate on the most pleasant spot on your drawing, on the moment when you felt the strongest joy of living. Close your eyes and try to live that feeling again, remember the details of the situation and recall them from your memory. Try to feel that deep inside you, now and here!* (Pause)
Sharing around the circle: *using a gesture, show us that feeling. Tell us, if you like, what caused that joy.*

5. **Confidence exercise:** *Let's stand up and stretch! Since we have been sitting for a long time, we could use a little exercise. It would be more interesting if we did it this way: let's make pairs (A and B). A will close his/her eyes and B will put his/her hand on A's shoulder and lead him/her around the room, wherever he/she wants and the way he/she wants, but in silence. Try to make the walk pleasant and interesting for the one you lead and not make him/her feel anything unpleasant, like bump into the others or hit something. Try to keep the game silent! It will make it more interesting.*
If they ask how they could guide without verbal instructions, the WL advises: *Try, find the way to speak with your hands, let your hand play the role of the words: move, stop, left, right, etc. After a while, when I give you a sign, you will change the roles.*

Sharing around the circle: *How did you feel playing both roles? What was more pleasant?* They are sitting in a circle and sharing how they felt during the walk and if they had confidence in their partners.

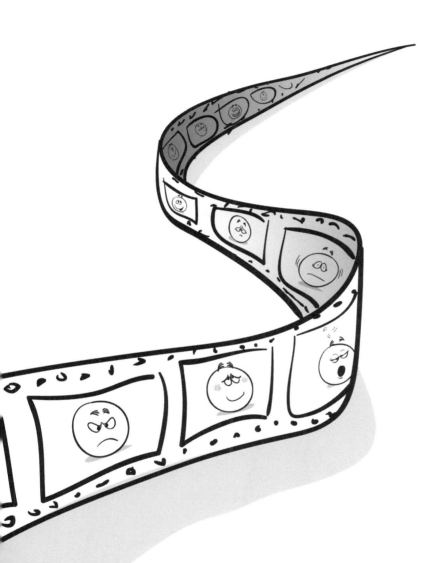

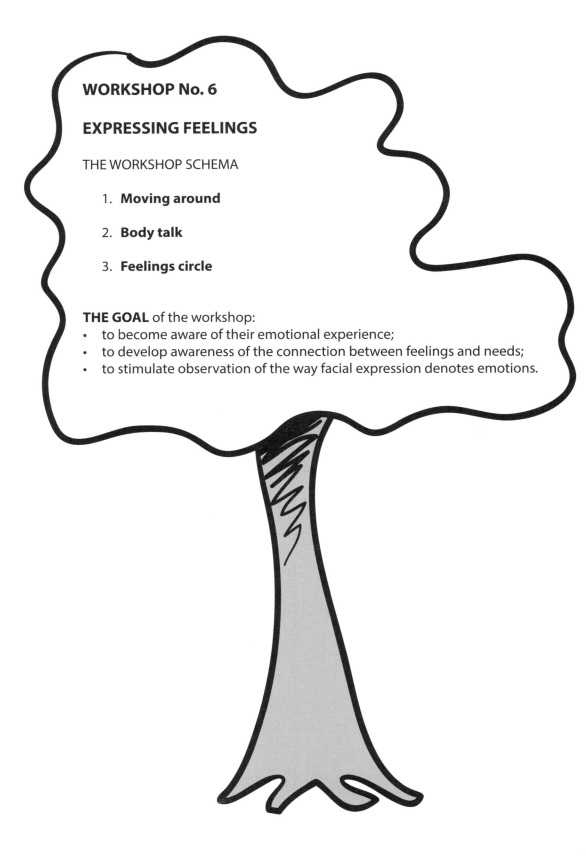

WORKSHOP No. 6

EXPRESSING FEELINGS

THE WORKSHOP SCHEMA

1. **Moving around**

2. **Body talk**

3. **Feelings circle**

THE GOAL of the workshop:
- to become aware of their emotional experience;
- to develop awareness of the connection between feelings and needs;
- to stimulate observation of the way facial expression denotes emotions.

EXPRESSING FEELINGS

1. **Moving around:** All participants stand in a circle. The WL says: *When I give you a sign, you start walking around the room. Think now of the path you follow. Then imagine that you are tired. How would you walk if you were tired? Well, start: tired...* (30 sec) *now as if you were angry...* (30 sec)*... now scared...* (30 sec.) *sad...* (30 sec) *now in a silly way...* (30 sec) *and now joyfully...* (30 sec) NOTE: Pay attention to nonverbal signs of anxiety: if children keep stiff while moving, if keep their fists tight, if they scratch themselves or suck their fingers.
They sit down, back in a circle.

2. **Body talk:** they are divided into 5 groups of "researchers" of body talk. Each group is choosing one feeling to focus on. The choice could be random (drawing cards with the name of the feeling out of a box), by decision of the WL or of the participants. Their task is to describe in detail (and draw) body talk: the body signs by which they recognize if someone is tired, afraid, sad, angry, joyful, in love. Encourage them to make humorous presentations, but keep the facts. Each group has 2 minutes to present their report, and they will have to designate the one who will present the results of the research. Presentation of the reports.

3. **Feelings circle:** *Close your eyes and pay attention to the way you feel now. Try to imagine that all your feelings, all the emotions you had for the last few days, are in one circle. How much space, what color and place would each of them take? Express that on the paper, using lines, colors and shapes that suit your recent feelings!*
While they are drawing the WL asks: *What is the structure of the circle? Are*

the borders clear or blurred? Is there anything that dominates?

WL comments: *Our feelings are messengers, informing us about something very important - our needs. If our needs are met we have pleasant feelings, if not - the feelings are unpleasant. They guide us to become aware of the need and to do something to meet the need.*

Task: *now try to connect every feeling that you have experienced in the circle with the need that feeling is informing you about.*

Sharing around the circle: *What is there in your feelings circle? What is the relationship between those feelings and needs? What needs are met / not met? How do the feelings change: suddenly, gradually? What does it depend on?*

Sharing around the circle: about the types and causes of mood changes.

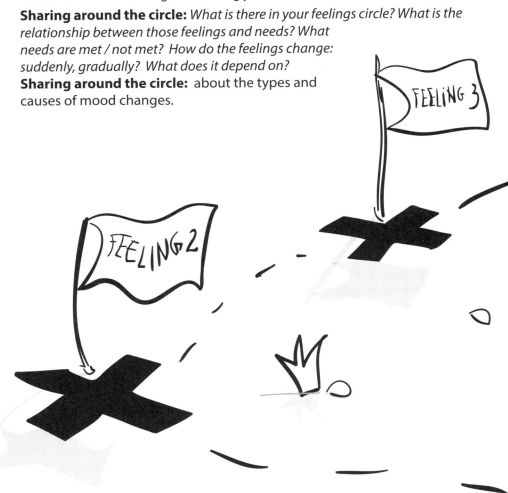

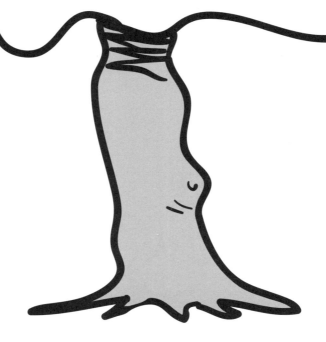

WORKSHOP No. 7

HOW DO WE COMMUNICATE OUR FEELINGS

THE WORKSHOP SCHEMA

1. **Mirror of feelings**

2. **Communicating feelings with the back of your body**

3. **Communicating feelings with words**

4. **Connection between feelings and needs**

5. **Confidence exercise: rocking**

THE GOAL of the workshop:
- to become aware of their emotional experience;
- to become aware of the connection between feelings and needs;
- to become aware of the different ways of communicating feelings;
- to stimulate communication of their feelings.

HOW DO WE
COMMUNICATE OUR FEELINGS

1. Exercise in pairs - **Mirror of feelings:** A is to change the expression on his face, expressing that way different emotions, and B is to imitate him simultaneously, as if he were A's reflection in the mirror. After 2-3 minutes they switch roles.
   Note: they are supposed to use neither hands nor anything else, only their face.
   Sharing around the circle: *How did it feel to play either of these roles? What did you like? What did you dislike? What was harder to do?*
   COMMENT: *The exercise is not only a good gymnastic for the face, but also helps us to become aware of how many muscles take part in our feelings, how many expressions our face can produce and what a wealth that is. We become aware not only of our facial expressions but also more sensitive in reading the signals other people send.*

2. **Communicating feelings with the back of your body:** Pairs are sitting back to back, touching each other all over their back. A is to communicate his feelings to B only by using his/her back. When the transmission is over, A says: "I'm over!" and writes down what the feeling was, without letting B see what was written. B makes his guess and writes down the feeling he received. Then A tries to convey three other feelings of his/her choice. He/she can choose whatever feeling or manner to show it using the back. When they finish this round of four feelings, they change roles.
   Sharing around the circle: *Did you succeed in recognizing the feelings? How did you feel during the exercise?*

3. **Communicating feelings with words:** The children are working in groups of three. Each group has the task to write as many adjectives denoting feelings as they can for 5 minutes. WL is gives an example: "joyful". Each group designates a representative to present their list of adjectives to the others.

   Presentation of the list: WL writes on the board every adjective and its frequency of appearance. WL comments on the richness of the list of adjectives, differentiating the words expressing feelings from words expressing judgment and not feeling, such as the word "neglected" or those denoting reactions without specifying feelings such as "smiling", etc.

4. **Connection between feelings and needs**: WL points out that pleasant feelings are connected with satisfied needs, and unpleasant feelings with unsatisfied needs.

   WL suggests playing a guessing game: everybody is invited to guess the needs connected to the feelings written on the board. Children are working individually and write down their guesses.

   Sharing around the circle: WL reads the words expressing feelings one by one, while the children make their guess of the needs. WL points out that one feeling could be connected with different needs.

5. **Confidence exercise: rocking**

They play this game in groups of three. Two of the children are standing face-to-face, the third one in the middle, and they have to rock him gently between them. The third should close his eyes and let them rock him. They push him gently, holding him by the shoulders. In the beginning they are very close, they can slowly make the distance grow, still staying in the zone of pleasant and safe rocking.

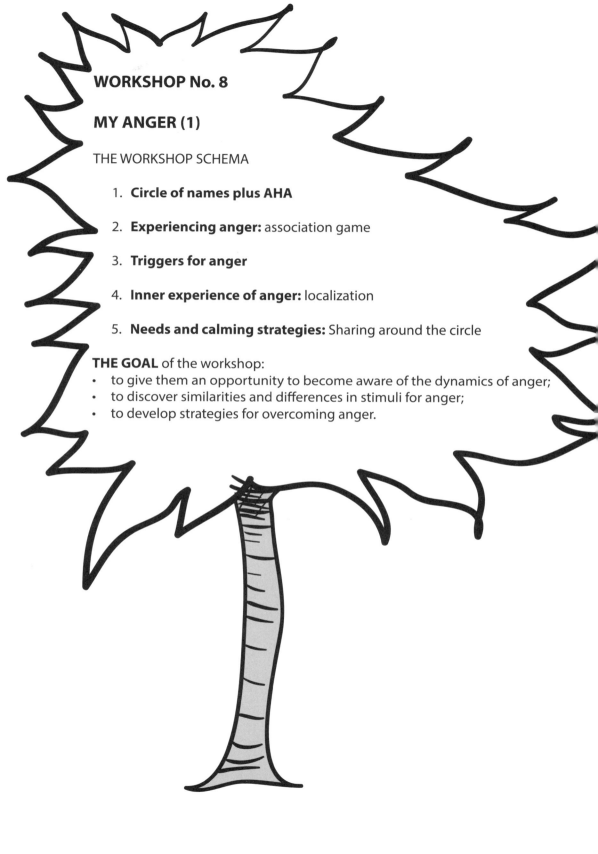

WORKSHOP No. 8

MY ANGER (1)

THE WORKSHOP SCHEMA

1. **Circle of names plus AHA**

2. **Experiencing anger:** association game

3. **Triggers for anger**

4. **Inner experience of anger:** localization

5. **Needs and calming strategies:** Sharing around the circle

THE GOAL of the workshop:
- to give them an opportunity to become aware of the dynamics of anger;
- to discover similarities and differences in stimuli for anger;
- to develop strategies for overcoming anger.

WORKSHOP No. 8

MY ANGER (1)

1. **Circle of names:**
   - *Cry out your name, as loud as you can, sharply!*
   - *Cry out your name and add a loud, sharp "Aha!"*

2. **Experiencing anger:** An association game around the circle asking children to quickly continue a sentence initiated by the WL:
   - *I am angry as a...*
   - *When I am angry, I feel like (doing)...*

3. **Triggers for anger:** *Try to remember some situation, thing, event or person that triggered your anger. Recall the details of that experience: who was there, where were you, what was the facial expression of the person, etc.*
   Sharing around the circle: *What are the triggers of your anger?*

4. **Inner anger experience:** localization.
   We are all sometimes angry or even mad. Close your eyes and try to remember how it is for you when you are angry. Pay attention to your reaction: physical sensation of anger, where in the body did it start to grow, how was it spreading, where did it come to by the end?
   Draw a contour of your body, and try to "map" your experience of anger: where does it start, how does it spread, find the right color, intensity, size for your experience of anger.
   Sharing around the circle: *Where in your body do you feel the anger? Where does it start? How does it spread? Where does it come to?*
   The children present and comment on their drawings.

5. **Calm down strategies:** *When you are angry, what do you need? How do you regain your calm? What do you do? What are your calming strategies? How do you calm yourself most easily?* Make the children describe the turning point, the crucial but so often not conscious moment of connection with a need.
   Sharing around the circle: needs and calming strategies.
   WL writes down all the needs and strategies on a big sheet of paper, each of them a short message-like, kind of calming down formula such as: Breathe slowly! Take a shower!
   In the end the group will have a poster listing their calming strategies.

WORKSHOP No. 9

MY ANGER (2)

THE WORKSHOP SCHEMA

1. **Sound of anger**

2. **Draw your anger**

3. **Angry thoughts**

4. **Expectations from the others**

5. **When we are mad what can we do** to express ourselves fully, but not to hurt neither others nor ourselves?

THE GOAL of the workshop:
- to become aware of the mechanism of anger;
- to have the opportunity to express anger;
- to develop strategies for overcoming and not suppressing anger.

MY ANGER (2)

1. **Sound of anger:** *Find the sound or syllable that best expresses your anger. It could be a hissing sound like "sssss" or growling like " grrrr". Let's produce that sound together, each of us in his or her own way!*

2. **Draw your anger:** *Find a shape, color, or symbolic expression for it.*
   Wait until they have finished, and then ask them to title their drawing.
   Sharing around the circle: the children show, explain, tell about the titles of the drawings and then figure out mechanisms of their angry thoughts.

3. **Angry thoughts:** *Remember what you are thinking of, what is going on in your head before you get angry?*
   Sharing around the circle.
   WL comment: *We get angry when we think that someone should not do "it" to us, that "it" is not fair, or correct, and so on and so forth. We focus on what we do not want to happen and forget what we want, what we would like to happen. If only we would direct our attention to what we really want and think about how to get it, our anger would disappear.*

4. **Expectations from the others:** *What would you like others to do when you are mad, how you would like them to behave toward you? And what do they usually do?* **Sharing around the circle.**
   WL comment: during the exchange, when it is needed, focus children's attention on whether they communicate their feelings and if they do, how do they do it? Stress the difference between "I" and "You" messages ("I feel...", not "You make me feel.... "). The message of anger that begins with "You" is a signal of an attack. Do they give a chance to the others to help them by saying clearly what they are needing?

5. **When we are mad what can we do to express ourselves fully**, but not to hurt neither others nor ourselves?
   WL reminds them that the most efficient way to deal with anger is to

45

immediately divert attention from the angry thoughts, to focus on the need that is not met and to tell it to the other, then ask what the other can do to meet their need.

If this does not work they can try:

a. to **twist a towel** with anger,

b. to **hit the bed** with a towel or with the hands and cry out,

c. to sit down, breathe slowly, imagine that a **wave of relaxation** goes down from the top of your head enveloping you until it reaches your toes.

Some strategies they can try right away:

d. **Doodling**: give them papers to release their anger doodling madly (they can draw a thing/thought that makes them mad and then scrub over it or can crumple the paper and then throw it away as far as they can),

e. **Lion's roar**: ask them to kneel keeping their feet straight, then sit back on their heels with top of their toes touching the floor. Ask them to put their hands on their knees, then open their mouth, relax muscles of the face, stick out their tongue as far as possible and let the all the air out of their lungs in silence. Then repeat these motions screaming from the bottom of their lungs, like a lion.

WL comment: *The energy of anger is necessary and important for survival, but it is also important that it does not become destructive either for the others or for us. We have to learn to use that energy in a creative way, control it but not suppress it.*

Let's do some exercises for relaxing and accumulating energy:

1. *Stand up and pay attention to taking your usual position. Move your hands all over your body as if you were taking a shower, try to feel and touch the spots where you feel the tension. The neck and the shoulders are the usual places where you have problems. You can feel it by the tension in those muscles.*

2. *Turn your head around slowly from right to left, backwards, to the right, ahead, then repeat the other way round keeping your eyes closed. Imagine that your head is light as a balloon. Repeat the exercise with your eyes open, let your look wander as your head moves, don't focus on anything.*

3. *"Get off my back" exercise: Stand up with your feet apart and parallel, knees relaxed, relax you belly, buttocks, and shoulders, let your arms hang. Breathe evenly and relax you jaws. Lift your elbows to the height of your shoulders, spread your arms, and then pull them back with a sudden and strong move crying out "Get off my back!" Repeat the exercise several times trying to express your mood with your voice.*

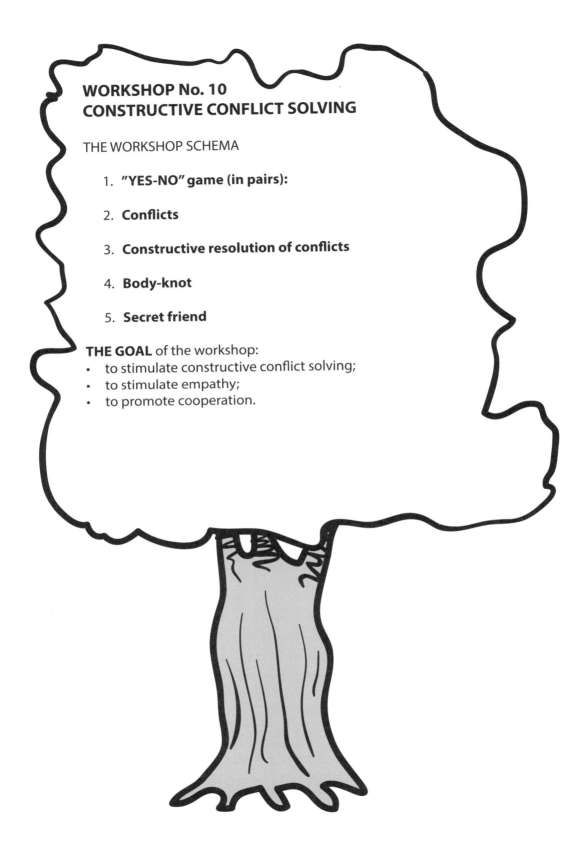

**WORKSHOP No. 10
CONSTRUCTIVE CONFLICT SOLVING**

THE WORKSHOP SCHEMA

1. **"YES-NO" game (in pairs):**

2. **Conflicts**

3. **Constructive resolution of conflicts**

4. **Body-knot**

5. **Secret friend**

THE GOAL of the workshop:
- to stimulate constructive conflict solving;
- to stimulate empathy;
- to promote cooperation.

CONSTRUCTIVE CONFLICT SOLVING

1. **"YES-NO" game (in pairs)**: A keeps saying YES and tries to make B also say YES, while B keeps on saying NO and tries to make A say NO, too. They are free to use all nonverbal tricks and strategies of persuasion. All pairs are standing in two rows, As facing Bs, and all speaking at the same time.

   Sharing around the circle: Did they succeed? How?

   WL comment: *Sometimes it is difficult for us to understand each other because we do not want to accept that the other can have another viewpoint, different from ours. Like in the story about the two men looking at number 6 written on the floor; one looks at it from one side and sees a 6 while the other standing on the opposite side sees a 9. One states that the number is 6, the other that it is 9, and each of them thinks that he is the only one speaking the truth. They can even fight about it thinking that they are right. All that is needed to solve the conflict is that one of them says: "Let me see what it looks like from your side!" Then both will know much more than they knew before.*

2. **Conflicts**: *Remember a situation when you were in a conflict with someone relatively close to you. Write down on a piece o paper who the person was and what was it that he/she said that made you angry as well as what your response was. Describe in few words how the conflict ended.* Encourage them to give the essence of the conflict, to write it as a script for a short play and, in order to encourage them to be frank, tell them that they will not have to sign the papers. They should describe the conflicts and put the papers in a box.

   WL invites two children to volunteer acting in the short play about the conflict. They pick up a paper from the box and act the conflict as written in the "script".

WL comment: *Our conflicts usually end up in one of the following ways:*
- *one wins and the other loses;*
- *they both lose;*
- *they reach a compromise in which both lose a lot and get very little.*

Therefore, the unpleasant feelings stay untouched and remain a source of future conflicts. Yet, there is always a new solution that can be found, a solution that would satisfy both sides and make both sides win.

3. **Constructive resolution of conflicts**:

   We will now try to find a new, constructive and creative solution to the conflicts on your papers. We will try to look for a solution that would satisfy both sides. We will put ourselves in both positions and try to think following the "good for me and good for you" pattern, **consider the needs of both parties**, *and imagine what they could say or do so that the conflict is resolved to their mutual satisfaction.*

   The WL picks up one of the papers and reads it in a loud voice. Children work in pairs, and try to come up with a constructive solution for that conflict. Each pair acts what they see as a solution for that conflict.

   Sharing around the circle: How did they come to those solutions? What was their initial step? What tactics did they use? Are both sides really satisfied?

   If there are difficulties the WL encourages them to imagine other ways for the conflict to be solved. He asks them to think of the conflict as a comic situation and imagine that they are writing a script for a comedy, or imagine the arguing parties as characters of a fairy tale.

   The game lasts for as long as there is time for it and the WL keeps extracting new conflicts from the box. All that counts is allowing ten minutes for the closing activities.

4. **Body-knot**: the children make a circle and hold each others' hands, then try to make a knot without letting their hands go and passing under the arms of the others. When they cannot make any other moves, they try to untangle.

5. **Secret friend**: Write your name on a piece of paper and put it in the box together with the others. Now take one paper from the same box and silently read the name of the one whose secret friend you are going to be until the end of the 12th workshop. This means that you will send him/her a nice message or make a small present or something like that, but NOT let him/her know who you are. If you pick up your own name, put it back in the box, and choose another.

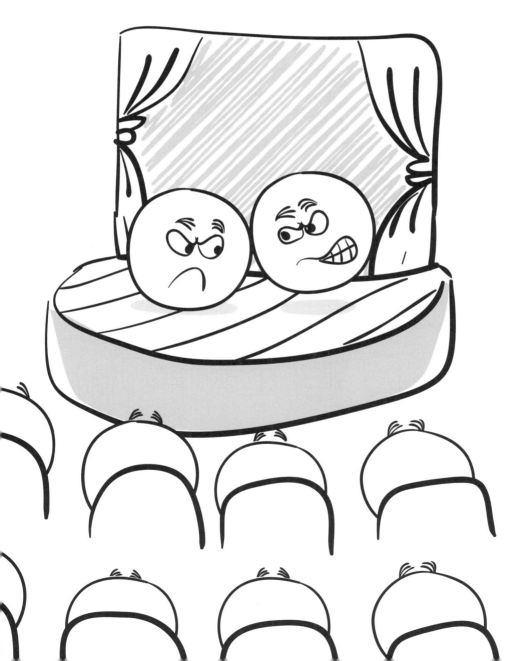

WORKSHOP No. 11

MEDIATING THE CONFLICT BETWEEN GIRLS AND BOYS

THE WORKSHOP SCHEMA

1. **Introductory game:** children suggest one

2. **Reasons for conflict between girls and boys.**
   Sharing in small groups.

3. **Detectives in action**

4. **The Labyrinth Game**

THE GOAL of the workshop:
- to learn to differentiate facts, feelings, needs of the parties in conflict;
- to learn to mediate in conflicts;
- stimulate constructive conflict solving.

WORKSHOP No. 11

MEDIATING THE CONFLICT BETWEEN GIRLS AND BOYS

1. **Introductory game:** children suggest one.

2. **Reasons for conflict between girls and boys. Sharing in small groups.** Children are divided into small groups of boys and of girls as they share and present what they have discovered about the reasons for conflicts between girls and boys.

3. **Detectives in action**
   WL: *We will now try to find a way to solve these conflicts so that everybody is satisfied. Some of you will be detectives/mediators, while the others will act as parts in the conflict.*
   Role-play: a conflict between a boy and a girl.
   The children are organized in groups of three: a boy, a girl and a mediator/detective. The boy and the girl choose the conflict they want to enact, and play their parts for 2-3 minutes. The mediator/detective listens silently. The WL gives instructions to the mediator/detective:
   Detectives in this case do not search for who is wrong and who is right, who made a mistake, or who should be punished. They just help with bringing to light what happened, what initiated their conflict, what both of them feel and need. They make use of the Detective's List that helps them to solve the case. Here is the Detective's List! (see appendix 1, page 55)
   The WL presents a poster with the Detective's list. He gives an example of how a detective works. The detective questions one and then the other party in the conflict:
   1. What happened, what started the conflict? Give me the facts!
       The Boy: She called me stupid!
       The Girl: He took my rubber!

2. How did you feel then?
   The Boy: I was angry!
   The Girl: I was angry, too!

3. What did you want?
   The Boy: I wanted her to lend me her rubber because I needed it. I wish she talked nicely, instead of calling me names!
   The Girl: I wanted him to ask for the rubber, not just grab it!

4. OK. What will make both of you happy now? What do you suggest?
   The Boy: Well, I can ask her nicely if she wants to give me her rubber!
   The Girl: I am sorry for calling you stupid. I didn't mean it! Really!

5. Are you both happy with this?
   The Boy and the Girl: Yes!!!

Mediation: The pairs act their conflict as the detectives tries to mediate.
Sharing around the circle: WL asks all the children if they liked this detectives' approach and if they thought it worked: Would it be possible to apply it in real life? Would it be helpful?

4. **The Labyrinth Game**
   One by one, blindfolded, children pass through the labyrinth made of the bodies of the other standing children whose bodies form a labyrinth. The blindfolded child has to find his way by groping, and the others help him by making sounds. When he gets close to the wall the child playing the wall calls: "Eeeeee!!!"

APPENDIX 1 for workshop No. 11

Make a photocopy of this page and cut it along the dashed line to make the Detective's list needed for workshop no. 11 (Detectives in action).

DETECTIVE'S LIST

1. WHAT HAPPENED, WHAT DID HE/SHE DO TO YOU? WHAT ARE THE FACTS?

2. HOW DID YOU FEEL?

3. WHAT DID YOU WANT?

4. SUGGESTIONS OF THE SOLUTION: WHAT CAN YOU DO NOW TO MAKE YOU BOTH HAPPY? WHAT DO YOU SUGGEST?

5. ARE YOU HAPPY WITH THE SOLUTION?

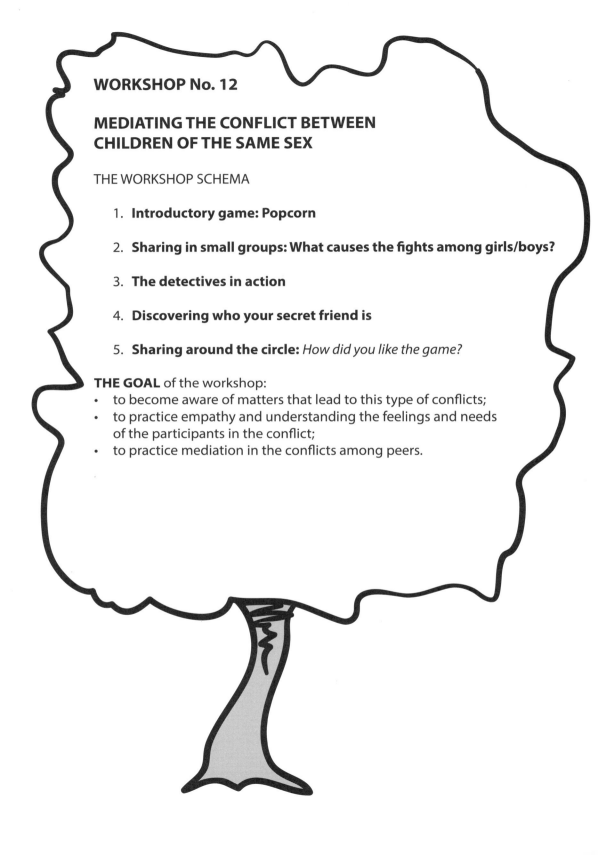

WORKSHOP No. 12

MEDIATING THE CONFLICT BETWEEN CHILDREN OF THE SAME SEX

THE WORKSHOP SCHEMA

1. **Introductory game: Popcorn**

2. **Sharing in small groups: What causes the fights among girls/boys?**

3. **The detectives in action**

4. **Discovering who your secret friend is**

5. **Sharing around the circle:** *How did you like the game?*

THE GOAL of the workshop:
- to become aware of matters that lead to this type of conflicts;
- to practice empathy and understanding the feelings and needs of the participants in the conflict;
- to practice mediation in the conflicts among peers.

MEDIATING THE CONFLICT
BETWEEN CHILDREN OF THE SAME SEX

1. **Introductory game: Popcorn**
   Children stand in a circle. The WL claps his/ her hands making the sound of the jumping popcorn; the child next to him/her repeats the clap faster, and so on. Play this game a couple of times in a row, each time accelerating the pace of clapping.
   WL comment: *In the previous workshop we discussed about the conflicts among girls and boys. We shall again have detectives/mediators help us solve this case of confilct among children of the same sex.*

2. **Sharing in small groups: What causes the fights among girls / boys?**
   The children are divided into small groups by sex; they talk to one another and then the representative of each group announces the conclusions of the group about the reasons for the fights among children of the same sex.

3. **The detectives in action**
   The role-play: Children are divided into groups of three (all of the same sex). Two of them are in conflict, and the third child is the mediator.
   Sharing around the circle: *How was it? Did you manage to understand each other? Did you notice that it is easier to solve the conflict when you are aware of the other person's feelings and wishes?*

4. **Discovering who your secret friend is**. All participants are sitting in a circle. One child enters the center of the circle and stands there with closed eyes. Then his secret friend joins him. The child in the center tries to guess who it is by touching the face of his secret friend, still with the eyes closed. After he discovered who the secret friend is, the first child stands back in the circle, and the secret friend closes his eyes, and gets to guess who his friend was; and so on.

5. **Sharing around the circle:** *How did you like the game? Was it hard to guess who the secret friend is? What did you do as a secret friend? Did you try to find out who your secret friend is? How did you feel whilst being a focus of their attention? What about the situation in which you had to think of ways of showing attention to someone else?*

WORKSHOP No. 13

MEDIATING THE CONFLICT BETWEEN PARENTS AND CHILDREN

THE WORKSHOP SCHEMA

1. **Introductory game: Let's be angry**

2. **Discussion**

3. **Sharing in small groups:** What causes conflicts between parents and children?

4. **The detectives in action**

5. **The opening of the fist**

6. **Discussion**

THE GOAL of the workshop:
- to become aware of the different modes of expressing anger;
- to become aware of matters that lead to the conflict between parents and children;
- to practice empathy and understanding the feelings and needs of the participants in the conflict.

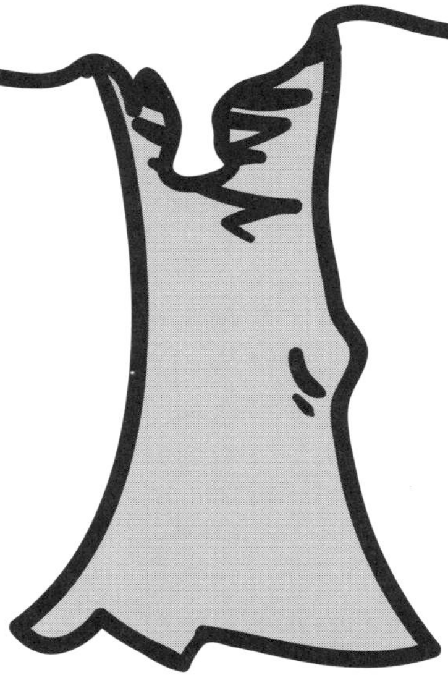

MEDIATING THE CONFLICT
BETWEEN PARENTS AND CHILDREN

1. **Introductory game: Let's be angry**
   The children move freely in the room. The WL tells them to remember how they felt when they were angry, to show what the expression on their faces was, what they were doing with arms and legs at the time, what they said and did, what they thought while they felt angry.
   Note: The leader pauses between commands giving children time to show what was asked of them.

2. **Discussion:** *Has your Mom or Dad ever happened to shout orders to clean your room or arrange your things in order, and you felt angry for being shouted at, and even more for having to do things that you are not really fond of doing?* **Sharing in the group.**
   The WL comment: *In the previous workshop, we talked about the conflicts among girls and boys. Today, we are going to deal with the reasons for arguments between parents and children. We are going to again have detectives help us solve the case.*

3. **Sharing in small groups:** *What causes conflicts between parents and children?*
   Children are divided into small groups. Girls and boys are mixed and they talk among themselves. The representative of each group announces the conclusions of the group regarding the causes for arguments between parents and children.

4. **The detectives in action**
   Role-play: the argument between parents and children.
   The children are divided into groups of three: Mom/Dad + the child + the detective/mediator. They choose the argument they want to enact. They argue while the detective/mediator listens silently.
   After about three minutes, the leader asks the children what they thought about the argument and how they felt while they talked in that manner.
   Sharing in the group.

The mediation: The pairs re-enact the conflict and the detectives try to mediate. They use the detectives' list of questions (Appendix 1) and try to help both sides state their feelings clearly, listen to each other, understand each other's feelings and needs, and discover what they can do to make both of them happy.

Sharing around the circle: The mediator of each group announces the conclusions of the group process: How was it? Did parents and children manage to understand each other?

5. **The opening of the fist**. The children are arranged in pairs, facing each other. The leader asks them to choose who will be no.1, and who will be no.2. Then, he instructs no.1s to clench the fist of their right hand. No.2s have the task to open the No.1s' fists.

The WL gives the children a couple of minutes to try to perform this task on their own, and then asks: *Has it occurred to any of you to ask your friend kindly to open his/her fist?*

The WL reminds the children that the instructions for the game do not state that the fist should opened by force. The WL points out that it is easier to do something by asking gently than by force.

6. **Discussion**. The leader asks all the children what they have learnt in the workshop, and if it seems to them that they are able to understand their parents better now? **Sharing in the group.**

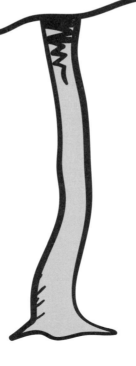

WORKSHOP No. 14

FEAR (1)

THE WORKSHOP SCHEMA

1. **Suspense walk**

2. **Experiencing fear**, an **association game** around the circle

3. **What makes one fear**

4. **Inner experience of fear: localization**

5. **Strategies against fear**

6. **Massage in a circle**

THE GOAL of the workshop:
- to give the children the opportunity to express and share fears;
- to develop strategies to overcome those fears.

FEAR (1)

1. **Suspense walk**: They all find a place in the room and stand there keeping some 40 - 60 cm distance between them. They close their eyes and start walking around, wherever they want. They do that in silence, keeping their arms close to their body. When they hear you say "*Stop!*" they freeze and, without touching, keeping their eyes closed, they try to guess how many children there are around them and how far away they are. Help them by saying: *Try to guess if there is anybody behind you, on your left, on your right, in front of you! Do not open your eyes!* After about two seconds they can open their eyes and verify the correctness of their guesses. The game is repeated two times.

   Pay attention to the way they move, how self-confident they seem to be, if they crowd together or move freely, if they touch each other, or hold their arms in front of them, if they giggle or whisper! In short, try to notice if there is any sign of anxiety.

   Sharing around the circle: *How did you feel during the walk? Did you feel any fear and if you did, fear of what? Was your guess correct?*

2. **Experiencing fear**, an **association game** around the circle: *Quickly complete the sentence!*

   I am scared like a...

   I got (adverb).... with fear.

   When I am scared, I feel like... (doing)

3. **What makes one fear**: *Close your eyes and try to think of situations, creatures, things, events or persons that make you afraid!*
   Sharing around the circle: *What are you afraid of? What do you fear the most? What do you need then?*

4. **Inner experience of fear: localization**. *Draw a contour of a human body!*

Try to draw your fear in it! Where is it? Is it in one place or it spreads? What colour is it? How strong is it? Try to express that using lines and your own symbols.
Sharing around the circle: *How and where do you feel fear?*
The children show their drawings and explain them.

5. **Strategies against fear:** *How do you cope with fear? What strategies do you use to deal with the fears that inhibit you? What do you do to overcome it?*
Sharing around the circle.

6. **Massage in a circle**. Children are standing in a circle and everyone is massaging the neck and the back of the child in front of him/her.

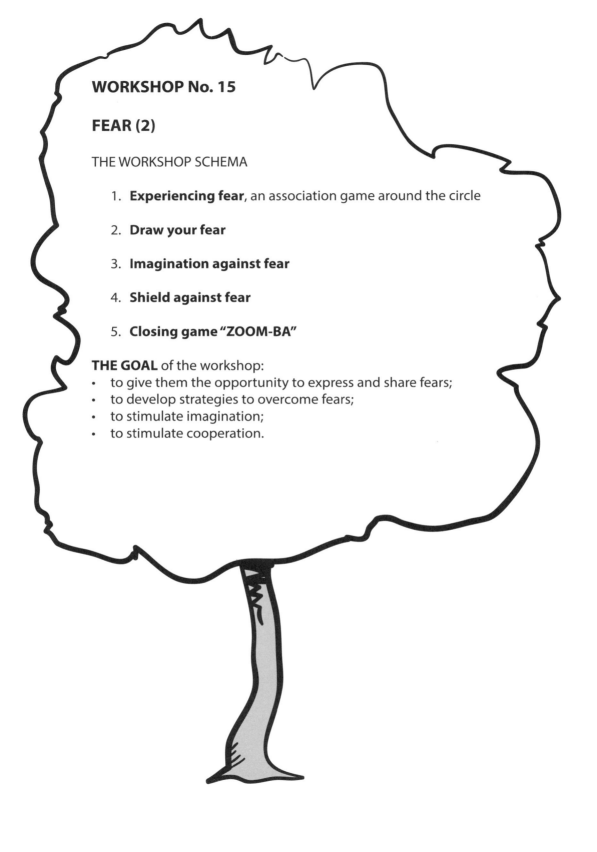

WORKSHOP No. 15

FEAR (2)

THE WORKSHOP SCHEMA

1. **Experiencing fear**, an association game around the circle

2. **Draw your fear**

3. **Imagination against fear**

4. **Shield against fear**

5. **Closing game "ZOOM-BA"**

THE GOAL of the workshop:
- to give them the opportunity to express and share fears;
- to develop strategies to overcome fears;
- to stimulate imagination;
- to stimulate cooperation.

WORKSHOP No. 15

FEAR (2)

1. **Experiencing fear**, an **association game** around the circle: *Quickly complete the sentence:*

   When I am scared, I feel like...(doing)

2. **Draw your fear**: Find the right shape, color, of symbolic presentation of your fear. After children have finished their drawing ask them to give a name to that drawing.
   Sharing around the circle: Showing, naming and explaining the drawings

3. **Imagination against fear**: *We will now use our imagination to overcome fear. It is easy because our mind knows how to get rid of the things it created. When I say 'get rid' I refer to that kind of fear that paralyses and depresses us. Yet, there are fear reactions that help us get alert and avoid danger: For example, a motor car horn will scare us, but prompt a sudden protective movement.*
   Sit comfortably, with your feet relaxed on the floor, arms relaxed, and palms on your knees. Find a comfortable position to hold your head. Relax your shoulders. Take it easy! Try to find the most comfortable position!
   Close your eyes. Breathe evenly: breathe in and count to three, breathe out and count to three. Feel the wave of relaxation flowing down from the top of your head, in a spiral, enveloping you and making you feel calm. Relax!!!
   All the sounds that you hear around are like a magic halo sheltering you. You absorb into that halo every new sound you hear. There is no sound that can disturb you.
   Feel how that relaxing wave spreads. Feel the tension disappear slowly, feel your whole body relax. The relaxing wave envelops you completely and makes you feel calm and peaceful.

   a) **Fear objectification**: *Imagine your fear as a creature... Pay attention to how it looks like, what form does it take… what its size is... Ask it why it is here? Ask it what you can do to make it go away? Listen very carefully to what it says!*

b) *Now imagine your fear in a diminished, ridiculous form... Make the changes in the projection in order to make the picture funny, amusing... Remember what changes you made....*

c) *Now try to set up your own assistant, helper who/which would deal with all the things that make you unnecessarily afraid... It could be a real or imaginary creature or thing... or a program... It is important that you think of a way to start it...*

e) *Now imagine that your mind is free of fears and anxieties, calm and full of energy.*

Open your eyes!

Sharing around the circle: *How did you like the relaxation exercise? What does your fear look like? What does it say? How can you get rid of it? Did you succeed in making it funny? How? Who/what is your assistant? How does it work?*

4. **A Shield against fear**

Make groups of four. Each group will make a shield against fear. It should contain all the things that help us transform fear into creative, positive energy, all the things that free us from unnecessary fears, tensions, or pressures. The children are free to decide on the shape and elements of the shield. They can activate their helpers, or invent something new.

Give a large sheet of paper to each group. They will do this as they like it. They can decide together what they will draw in his/her corner of the paper. They can draw individually on an A4 paper format, and then fix it together on a larger paper.

Sharing around the circle: group representatives show the shields and explain them.

5. **Closing game "ZOOM-BA"**: You say "Zoom!" and the one sitting next to you has to say "Zoom!" quickly and to pass the word to the person sitting next to him/her and so on, until somebody says "Ba!" Then "Zoom!" goes backwards, until somebody else says "Ba!" And so on and so forth.

WORKSHOP No. 16

SADNESS

THE WORKSHOP SCHEMA

1. **Circle of names:** *Say your name sadly*!

2. *What makes you sad?*

3. *What do you usually do when you are sad?*

4. **Inner experience of sadness:** localization

5. **Sharing around the circle:** *Do you cry easily?*

6. **Smile can change you inside**

7. **Modeling:** *Let us see how we can help each other feel better!*

8. **Closing game "OH-AH!"**

THE GOAL of the workshop:
- to give the children the opportunity to express and share sadness;
- to develop strategies to overcome sadness;
- to stimulate cooperation.

WORKSHOP No. 16

SADNESS

1. **Circle of names:** Say your name sadly!

2. **What makes you sad?** *Share with us one of your reasons to be sad.* **Sharing around the circle.**

3. **What do you usually do when you are sad?** *Do you go somewhere looking for company or you would rather be alone? What kind of music do you listen to when you are sad?*

4. **Inner experience of sadness:** localization. *Where is your sorrow located? Where do you feel the sadness in your body? Does it stay in one place or does it spread? And if it spreads through your body, where does it go?*
   The children draw a contour of human body and mark on it where and how they feel sadness.
   Sharing around the circle: *Where do you feel sadness? What does it look like?*
   They comment on their drawings. In the end the WL makes a summary of the similarities and differences in the way we experience sorrow.

5. **Sharing around the circle:** *Do you cry easily?*
   WL comment: *It is good to cry. Crying relaxes us and calms us down.*
   It is important to have time for sadness and for the other feelings, too.

6. **Smile can change you inside:** *We will now try something that can help us feel better. It is well known that our face mirrors our feelings. A researcher wanted to explore what happens if we deliberately change our face expression. Will it cause a change in our mood, too? He found out it does. Would you like to try? ...OK, let's try it! Close your eyes and make up a happy, smiling face. Keep it up until I say: "It is all right".*
   Let the children do this for about a minute.
   Sharing around the circle: *Was our little experiment successful? How do you feel now?*

7. **Modeling**: *Let us see how we can help each other feel better! We will try to make that change go from the outside to the inside, as we did it by smiling.*
The children get into two groups: one group makes "sadness statues" by assuming their usual position when they are sad. The other group are "the sculptors" who have to turn them into "happy statues". Every sculptor is allowed to make only one change on the statue. He is free to decide whether he will change the position of the hand, leg, face, etc. When he makes a change on one figure, he moves on and makes it on the next one, too, and so on. When all the sculptors are through, they check what they had done, and if they are satisfied with their work. In the meantime the "statues" are motionless in the position the sculptors have put them.
Role shift: The statues become sculptors, and sculptors become statues, and the game is repeated.
Sharing around the circle: How was it for them in the role of a sculptor and a statue? Did they notice the change in the mood during modeling?

8. **Closing game "OH-AH!"** The children are in a circle, holding one another's hands. The WL starts squeezing gently the hand of the child on his right saying: "AH!" The squeeze and "AH!" go around the circle to the right. Then the WL sends "OH!" and a squeeze to his left., and "OH" starts going around the circle before the circle of "AH" is finished. The child who receives "AH " and "OH" at the same time needs to react quickly and send both in the right direction without breaking the circle. Mistakes make all the fun of this game!

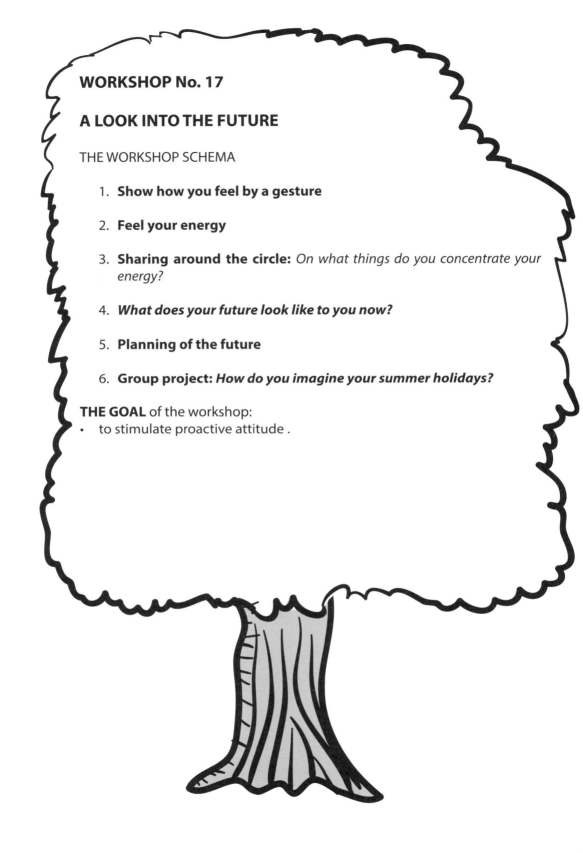

WORKSHOP No. 17

A LOOK INTO THE FUTURE

THE WORKSHOP SCHEMA

1. **Show how you feel by a gesture**

2. **Feel your energy**

3. **Sharing around the circle:** *On what things do you concentrate your energy?*

4. *What does your future look like to you now?*

5. **Planning of the future**

6. **Group project:** *How do you imagine your summer holidays?*

THE GOAL of the workshop:
· to stimulate proactive attitude .

A LOOK INTO THE FUTURE

1. **Show how you feel by a gesture**: one child shows and than everybody repeats the movement (body position and facial expression) simultaneously; they have to mirror and reflect the feeling of the person they imitate.

2. **Feel your energy:** *Hold your hands in front of you with palms facing each other and leaving 30 - 40 cm between them. Then slowly bring them closer, to a distance of about 10 cm. Repeat this a couple of times, until you feel the energy flow. It is as if you are holding a ball that gives you thrills.*

3. **Sharing around the circle**: *On what things do you concentrate your energy? Do you make plans about what you are going to do daily/weekly? Who decides on what will happen next - you or the circumstances?*

4. ***What does your future look like to you now?*** *Draw your own future, using shapes, lines, colors, or your own symbols!*
   Sharing around the circle: *What does your future look like?*
   Presenting and commenting on the drawings.

5. **Planning of the future**: *In order to concentrate our energy on the things we want we should make a plan. First, you are going to relax. Sit comfortably, with your feet on the floor, relaxed. Arms are relaxed, palms on your knees. Find a comfortable position to hold your head. Relax your shoulders. Take it easy. Try to find the most comfortable position.*
   Close your eyes. Breathe evenly: breathe in and count to three, breathe out and count to three. Feel the wave of relaxation going down from the top of your head, like a spiral, enveloping you and making you feel calm. Relax!
   All the sounds that you hear around are like a magic halo sheltering you. You absorb into that halo every new sound you hear. There is no sound that can disturb you.

Feel how that relaxing wave spreads. Feel the tension disappear slowly, feel your whole body relax. The relaxing wave envelops you completely and makes you feel calm and peaceful.

- *Choose one goal important to you now, choose what is important for you to accomplish;*
- *Imagine in detail what you can do to accomplish it, what are the steps leading to that outcome;*
- *Choose a helper that will support you in accomplishing it;*
- *Imagine a positive outcome, your goal accomplished, positive feelings about it;*
- *Imagine how the persons you care about would react to your success;*
- *Come back to the present moment, slowly;*
- *Open your eyes.*

Sharing around the circle: *How did you feel during this exercise? What plan did you choose? (If they want to talk about it) Who is your helper?*

6. *Now we will try to make a* **group project**. *The subject is:* **How do you imagine your summer holidays?** *Show it in five live pictures. Just like slides.*
   The children do this in groups of 4-5. Each group agrees on the story they are going to show. Give 10 minutes for preparing what and how they want to present in the five pictures. Then the groups perform. And the performance goes like this: children in the audience close their eyes and the actors take their positions for the first picture. The audience opens their eyes when the WL gives a sign, they take a look and the WL gives them a sign to close their eyes again. The group makes a second picture, and so on. In the end, the audience members interpret what they saw. Then the next group performs.

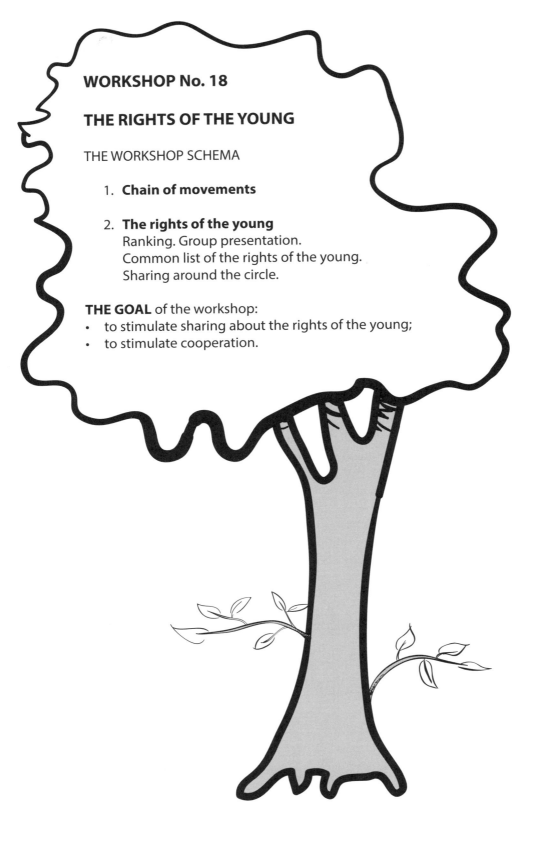

WORKSHOP No. 18

THE RIGHTS OF THE YOUNG

THE WORKSHOP SCHEMA

1. **Chain of movements**

2. **The rights of the young**
   Ranking. Group presentation.
   Common list of the rights of the young.
   Sharing around the circle.

THE GOAL of the workshop:
- to stimulate sharing about the rights of the young;
- to stimulate cooperation.

WORKSHOP No. 18

THE RIGHTS OF THE YOUNG

1. **Chain of movements:** everybody stands in the circle and has to repeat the movements of the person standing on his/her left. The WL starts and they repeat one after another:
   - snap you fingers
   - clap your thighs
   - clap your thighs and stomp with your feet
   - stomp with your feet
   - freeze

2. **The rights of the young**
   Write down nine rights you consider the most important for young people of your age. Encourage the children not to force themselves to put it in a special way, but to say it as simply as they want, for example, "to go out where they want".
   Ranking: in groups of 4 - 5 they rank the rights they have written. They decide which of the written rights would take the first place, which one they think is the most important, and then which one would take the second place, etc. They follow the pattern:

   <pre>
           1
         2   3
       4   5   6
         7   8
           9
   </pre>

   Group presentation: Each group presents its scheme and explains the reasons of such a choice.
   Common list of the rights of the young: together they make one final list of nine basic rights of the young.
   Sharing around the circle: *Do you feel deprived of some rights? Which rights of yours are respected? How can you defend and keep your rights? What needs are protected by these rights?*

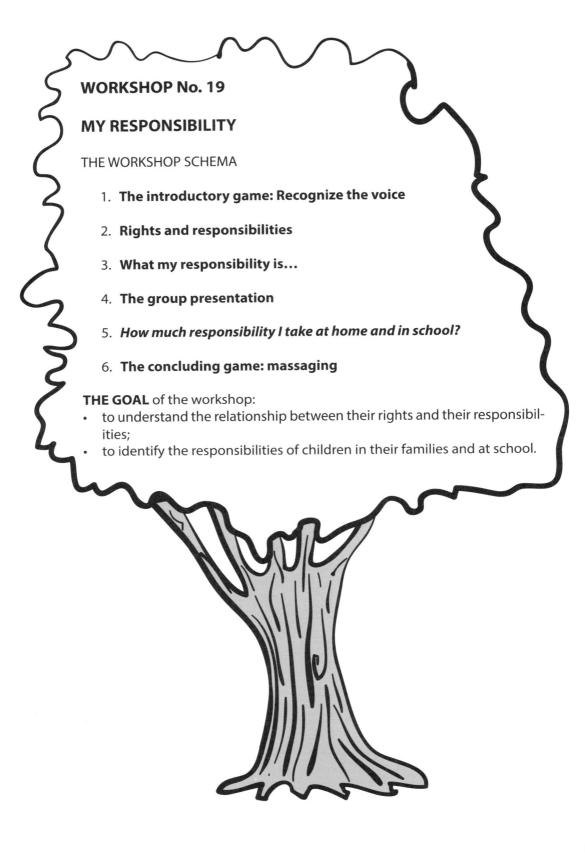

WORKSHOP No. 19

MY RESPONSIBILITY

THE WORKSHOP SCHEMA

1. **The introductory game: Recognize the voice**

2. **Rights and responsibilities**

3. **What my responsibility is...**

4. **The group presentation**

5. *How much responsibility I take at home and in school?*

6. **The concluding game: massaging**

THE GOAL of the workshop:
- to understand the relationship between their rights and their responsibilities;
- to identify the responsibilities of children in their families and at school.

MY RESPONSIBILITY

1. **The introductory game: Recognize the voice**.
   One of the children volunteers to sit in the centre of the circle, blindfold. The WL should go around the circle and touch a child who should speak to the one sitting in the middle of the circle in an altered voice. The task of the child sitting in the center of the circle is to recognize the voice. When the child succeeds, the one whose voice has been recognized enters the circle to do the same thing, blindfold.

2. **Rights and responsibilities**: The WL informs the children that each right they get draws a certain responsibility with regard to the manner in which that right should be used, always taking in consideration the welfare of others as well as of ourselves. For example, the right to speak freely does not mean that we should insult people or ridicule them, but that we should consider each other's feelings when we speak freely.

3. **What my responsibility is...**
   The WL prepares in advance some notes with children's rights, each note containing one right. Each child in the small group considers the right on the note they had drawn and tries to determine the responsibilities that the particular right implies. They are free to choose the way in which they will present their conclusions as a group. They could prepare a sketch in which one of the rights is used with and without responsibility. The WL goes from one group to the other giving help, if needed.

4. **The group presentation**: Each of the small groups has 5 minutes to present its work to the other children.

5. *How much responsibility I take at home and in school?*
   The children are divided into two groups, and are arranged in such a way that each of the two groups faces the other, lined up by the two opposite

walls in the classroom. The WL tells them to imagine that the middle line between them (possibly drawn with chalk) marks maximum of responsibility, and the place where they are standing marks no responsibility whatsoever.

When the WL asks the question: "*How much responsibility do you take at home?*", the children are supposed to find their spot in the space between the wall and the line marking the best possible case. Each child takes as many steps as he/she thinks appropriate, not looking at the other children. When the children have taken their places, the WL asks: "*What is your responsibility at home?*" After that, the leader asks the question: "*What are your responsibilities at school?*" **Sharing in the group**.

6. **The concluding game**: Arranged in a circle, children massage the neck and back of the child standing in front of them.

WORKSHOP No. 20

WHEN CHILDREN VIOLATE CHILDREN'S RIGHTS

THE WORKSHOP SCHEMA

1. **The acts of mockery**

2. **The investigators in action**

3. **The presentation of the group reports**

4. **The detectives in action**

5. **The presentation of group reports**

6. **The mutual support**

THE GOAL of the workshop:
- to evoke different types of situations in which abuse, mockery and violence against other children is committed;
- to learn to understand the causes of such behavior;
- to learn the ways in which they can protect themselves.

WHEN CHILDREN VIOLATE CHILDREN'S RIGHTS

1. **The acts of mockery.** The child who remembers some gestures of mockery shows them, and then, the other children repeat the gesture.
    Sharing around the circle: *How do you feel when someone mocks at you? What is your usual course of action in that case? Does that make you feel better?*

2. **The investigators in action**. The children are divided into groups, and each of the groups has the task to investigate all the possible ways of children behavior in which children's rights are broken. The leader reminds them that aside from mocking at one's physical appearance, origin, or name, children's rights violation could also be: exclusion from playing, pushing and shoving, extortion of one's possession or school lunch, gossiping, threatening, swearing, etc. Each of the groups has the task of making a list of such behavior and choosing the one they consider the worst violation of children's rights. Remind the children that they have the right to be respected for who they are, the right to privacy, and the right to be protected from abuse.

3. **The presentation of the group reports**. Each of the groups states the findings of their investigations. The WL writes the modes of behavior on the blackboard and their frequency of occurrence in the reports of the small groups of children.

4. **The detectives in action**. Divided in small groups, the children have the task of choosing some of the behaviors from the blackboard and trying to discover why children act so. How does the child behaving in that way feel? What does he/she need, and what does he/she miss? Remind the children to attempt to walk in the shoes of the child that behaves in that way.

The second task implies thinking of ways in which such a child could be helped to change behavior of the kind. Remind the children that everyone wants to be valued and respected, as well as accepted by his/her peers.

5. **The presentation of group reports**. Each of the groups states their findings and the ways in which they could help the child who behaves in an abusive manner.

6. **The mutual support.** The WL announces that they will practice giving and receiving appreciation. Giving and receiving appreciation is as important as food. The children speak to the one standing on their right side: "The thing I like about you is…"

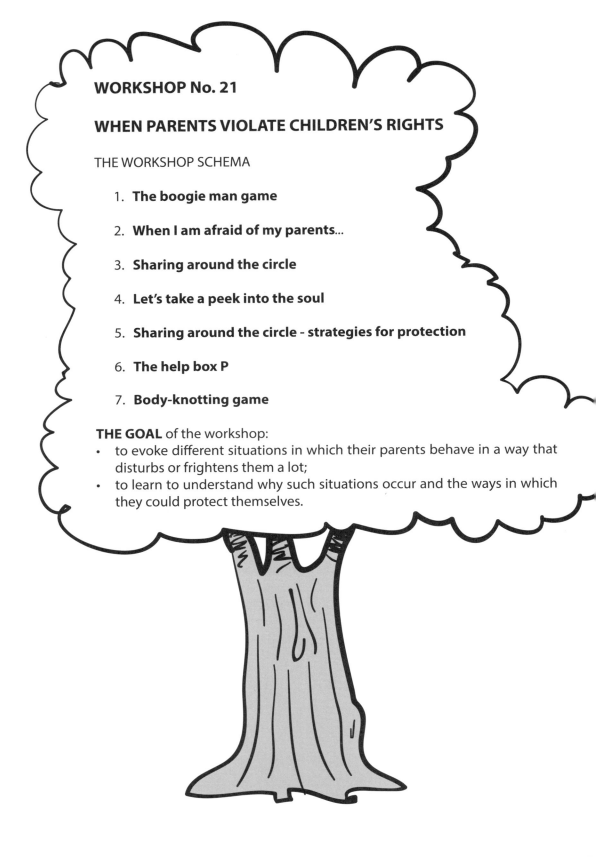

WORKSHOP No. 21

WHEN PARENTS VIOLATE CHILDREN'S RIGHTS

THE WORKSHOP SCHEMA

1. **The boogie man game**

2. **When I am afraid of my parents...**

3. **Sharing around the circle**

4. **Let's take a peek into the soul**

5. **Sharing around the circle - strategies for protection**

6. **The help box P**

7. **Body-knotting game**

THE GOAL of the workshop:
- to evoke different situations in which their parents behave in a way that disturbs or frightens them a lot;
- to learn to understand why such situations occur and the ways in which they could protect themselves.

WHEN PARENTS VIOLATE CHILDREN'S RIGHTS

1. **The boogie man game**. The class is divided into groups. The child A tries to frighten the child B by making sounds, body movements and facial expressions. After 5 minutes, the roles are reversed.

2. ***When I am afraid of my parents:*** children draw the situations in which their parents behave in a way that scares or disturbs them; they attempt to present in the drawing what the parent does and in strip balloons they write what the parent says to cause fear or unease with the child.

3. **Sharing around the circle**. Every child shows his/her drawing and talks about the things that scare or disturb him/her.

4. **Let's take a peek into the soul**.
   The WL comment: *It is probably very hard for you to understand why your parents behave in such a way, and you want to be sure that they care about you, even when they act in that manner. Let us try to discover why the parents behave like that.* The WL lists each of the mentioned behaviors and helps the children understand how the parents feel (powerless, discontented, etc.) and what they actually want (respect, understanding, etc.)

5. **Sharing around the circle - strategies for protection**. *What can you do to protect yourself in such a situation?* The children exchange their own strategies.
   The WL suggests that they could tell their parents: *"Wait Mom/Dad, this scares me, I want to understand you!"*

6. **The help box P**. The leader suggests that they should make a box in the classroom in which they should put notes on which they write those hard for them to understand behaviors of their parents or other adults they deal with, which scare or disturb them, and which they are unable to understand. The leader makes a plan with the children about the date of the opening of the box, when they will try to understand together why the adults act in this manner and how they can protect themselves from such behavior.

7. **Body-knotting game**: the children make a circle and hold each others' hands, then try to make a knot without letting their hands go and passing under the arms of the others. When they cannot make any other moves, they try to untangle.

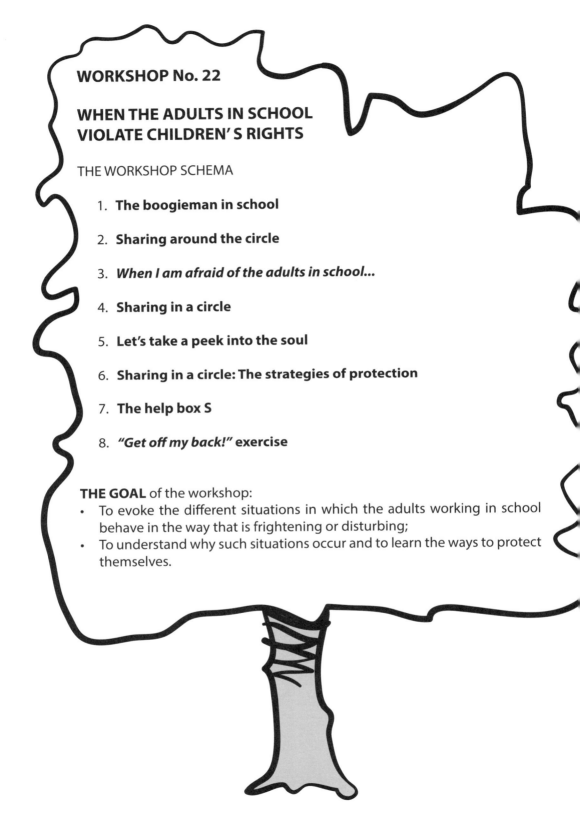

WORKSHOP No. 22

**WHEN THE ADULTS IN SCHOOL
VIOLATE CHILDREN'S RIGHTS**

THE WORKSHOP SCHEMA

1. **The boogieman in school**

2. **Sharing around the circle**

3. *When I am afraid of the adults in school...*

4. **Sharing in a circle**

5. **Let's take a peek into the soul**

6. **Sharing in a circle: The strategies of protection**

7. **The help box S**

8. *"Get off my back!"* **exercise**

THE GOAL of the workshop:
- To evoke the different situations in which the adults working in school behave in the way that is frightening or disturbing;
- To understand why such situations occur and to learn the ways to protect themselves.

WHEN THE ADULTS IN SCHOOL VIOLATE CHILDREN'S RIGHTS

1. **The boogieman in school**. The children move freely around the classroom. When the leader signals (for example, by clapping hands), the child tells the other child who happens to be near him "Shut up!" and they look him/her in the eyes. The WL chooses the sentences that the adults typically use to threaten the children in school, when the former feel powerless, try to regain the order in the classroom, or capture the children's attention for what they want to teach them.

2. **Sharing around the circle.** *How did you feel during the game? What are the most frightening sentences that teachers or other adults utter in school?*

3. ***When I am afraid of the adults in school...*** In groups of four, the children draw the situations in which the teacher or someone else behaves in a manner that frightens or disturbs them a lot. They attempt to draw what the adult does and to write in the balloon what he/she says that provokes fear or unease in the child. The WL should mention that those frightening things could be some gestures or actions without words.

4. **Sharing in a circle.** Each of the groups presents their drawings and explains what the things that frighten or disturbs them are.

5. **Let's take a peek into the soul**.
   The WL comment: *It is probably hard for you to understand why the adults behave like that and you want to be sure that they care about you, even in that type of situations. Let us try to discover why the adults behave in that manner.* The WL states each of the mentioned ways of behavior and helps the children discover how the adults feel (powerless, discontented, etc) and what they want (understanding, respect, attention, etc.)

6. **Sharing in a circle: The strategies of protection**. *What can you do to protect yourselves in such a situation?* The children exchange their own strategies.
   The workshop leader states that they can say: *"Stop, I'm really frightened by that, I want us to understand each other…"*

7. **The help box S**. The leader suggests that they should install a box in the classroom in which they will put the notes on which they will write all the behaviors of the adults in school that scare or disturb them, and which they are unable to understand. The leader makes a plan with the children about the date of the opening of the box, when they will try to understand together why the adults act in this manner and how they can protect themselves from such behavior.

8. ***"Get off my back!"* exercise**: *Stand up with your feet apart and parallel, knees relaxed, relax you belly, buttocks, and shoulders, let your arms hang. Breathe evenly and relax you jaws. Lift your elbows to the height of your shoulders, spread your arms, and then pull them back with a sudden and strong move crying out "Get off my back!" Repeat the exercise several times trying to express your mood with your voice.*

WORKSHOP No. 23

**WE ARE ALL DIFFERENT,
BUT OUR RIGHTS ARE THE SAME**

THE WORKSHOP SCHEMA

1. **The game: "The island (elimination)"**

2. **Sharing around the circle**

3. **The game: "The island (inclusion)"**

4. **Sharing around the circle**

5. **Sharing in small groups**

6. **The game: "Make a Rainbow"**

7. **Sharing in small groups**

THE GOAL of the workshop:
- to learn how to recognize the negative stereotypes, the situations in which some of the children get rejected by the group because they come from different social, ethnic or cultural layers of society;
- to learn how to understand the feelings of those who happen to be rejected in that way, and how to prevent such situations from occurring.

WORKSHOP No. 23

WE ARE ALL DIFFERENT,
BUT OUR RIGHTS ARE THE SAME

1. **The game: "The Island (elimination)"**. The leader spreads newspapers on the floor, which represent the islands between which the children are to "sail", and on which they are supposed to stand when the ML signals "Landing!" In the beginning, there should be enough newspapers for all the children to disembark onto. During the game, the leader removes islands one by one so that some of the children do not manage to land, so they leave the game.

2. **Sharing around the circle**: *How did you feel when they had to leave the game?*

3. **The game: "The island (inclusion)"**. The game is repeated, the children are supposed to stand on newspapers when the leader signals "Landing!" but this time their task is to take care that all of the children have a place to land. It can even be outside the island providing they hold each other's hands or are in any way connected with the ones standing on the islands. Again the WL removes islands one by one in order to make the task harder for all children.

4. **Sharing around the circle**: *How did you feel when you had to take care that everyone lands on an island?*

5. **Sharing in small groups**: *Are there any situations in which children may experience exclusion from the group? Why does this happen?*
   Each of the small groups states the results of the exchange.

6. **The game: "Make a Rainbow"**. The WL prepares some cards with circles of different colors (if there are 20 children, the leader makes 5 blue, 5 red, 5 green, 5 purple cards) in advance. Each child draws a card (cards are

turned so that children cannot see the color). When the WL gives his sign, the children are supposed to form groups, each of the groups should be made of differently colored cards.

The workshop leader's commentary: *In a rainbow, there is place for all the colors and that's why it looks so beautiful and appealing.*

7. **Sharing in small groups**: How can they change the mentioned situations of exclusion, so that everyone feels accepted?
All the small groups state the results of the exchange.

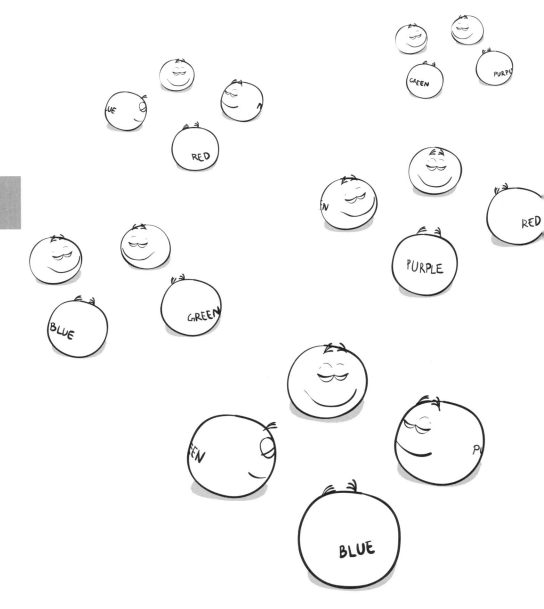

APPENDIX 2
for workshop No. 23

Make a photocopy of this page and cut it along the dashed lines to make the five 4-card sets needed for the workshop ("Make a rainbow" game).

RAINBOW CARDS

BLUE	GREEN	RED	PURPLE
BLUE	GREEN	RED	PURPLE
BLUE	GREEN	RED	PURPLE
BLUE	GREEN	RED	PURPLE
BLUE	GREEN	RED	PURPLE

WORKSHOP No. 24

THE VALUES

THE WORKSHOP SCHEMA

1. **The Game: "Boom and Bam".**

2. **I Can Do That**

3. **My Vow**

4. **Laughing**

THE GOAL of the workshop:
- to state their own actions which prove that they had accepted some of the mentioned values.
- to find new actions that could express these values.

THE VALUES

1. **The Game: "Boom and Bam"**.
   The children hold their hands in a circle. The WL sends the grip of the hand to the pupil on his right side, saying loudly "Boom". After a few moments, the grip is sent to the pupil on his/her left side with a loud "Bam". Each of the pupils has the task of carrying the grip of the hand and shout "Boom" or "Bam" to his or her neighbor in the circle. The game becomes interesting when "Boom" and " Bam" are sent to the same person, who has to transmit them to two persons at the same time…

2. **I Can Do That**. The WL prepares some cards with one of the values or virtues written on each of them (sincerity, honesty, good-heartedness, perseverance, eagerness, understanding, patience, kindness, fairness, bravery, calmness, independence, resoluteness, camaraderie, confidence in others, self-confidence, caring, creativity, tenderness, goodwill, gratitude, responsibility, strength, forgiveness, freedom of choice, harmony, compassion, love, generosity, support). Each of the children draws one of the cards and is supposed to remember some situation in his/her life when he or she had displayed that particular value, as well as to describe how and by what action. If a child is unable to think of that kind of situation on his/her own, the WL helps them.
   Sharing around the circle: What did they do to show that particular value?

3. **My Vow**. The leader gathers the cards, shuffles them and the children draw the cards again. Each of the children draws one card and is supposed to think of a new way to display the chosen value by his/her behavior. If a child is unable to remember, the leader helps.
   Sharing in a circle: What do they plan to do to display the chosen value.

4. **Laughing**. The children are arranged in two rows, facing each other (everyone has his or her pair in the other row). The children from one row try to make the children from the other row laugh, while the former tries to remain serious and calm. They change roles.

APPENDIX 3
for workshop No. 24

Make a photocopy of these two pages and cut them along the dashed lines to make the 30 cards needed for the workshop (I Can Do That).

VALUE / VIRTUE CARDS

sincerity	kindness
honesty	fairness
good-heartedness	bravery
perseverance	calmness
eagerness	independence
understanding	resoluteness
patience	camaraderie

confidence in others	strength
self-confidence	forgiveness
caring	freedom of choice
creativity	harmony
tenderness	compassion
goodwill	love
gratitude	generosity
responsibility	support

WORKSHOP No. 25

WHAT DO YOU DO, WHEN VALUES ARE VIOLATED?

THE WORKSHOP SCHEMA

1. **The Game - Show how you feel by using body language**

2. **This is my vote**

3. **The Gesture of Camaraderie**

THE GOAL of the workshop:
- To think about some of the situations in which the children violate some of the basic values;
- To learn to recognize the needs that drive children to behave in such a manner;
- To learn new ways to satisfy those needs, without violating the basic values.

I HATE
TREES

WHAT DO YOU DO, WHEN VALUES ARE VIOLATED?

1. **The Game** - *Show how you feel by using body language*. Everyone repeats the gestures, the body movements, or the facial expression at the same time. That entails that they have to observe the performer and mirror the feeling presented.

2. **This is my vote**. The leader marks three areas in the room with chalk. In one of the areas gather the children who support what is stated (PRO), in the other those who are against it (CON), and in the third those who are UNDECIDED. The leader states something and the children occupy the position expressing their attitude towards the statement. When all the children have decided on their position, the WL asks the children in all three groups what the reason for their decision was.

   Statement 1: "Whoever takes something that belongs to another person, is a thief."

   Statement 2: "There are no gossips in our class."

   Statement 3: "There is no excuse for lying."

   After sharing their thoughts about each and every of these statements, the WL tries to help the children understand the underlying reasons for such behavior, and they try together to think of a way to satisfy such needs without the violation of values.
   Sharing in the group.

3. **The Gesture of Camaraderie**. All of the participants send the gesture of camaraderie to the person standing on their left (shaking hands, kiss, etc.), who sends the gesture to the next person, and so on, until the gesture of camaraderie reaches the child which opened the circle.

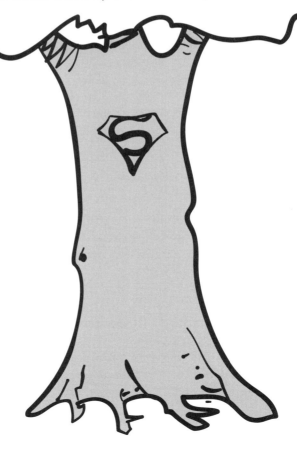

WORKSHOP No. 26

MY FAVORITE STORY/ COMIC/ MOVIE HERO

THE WORKSHOP SCHEMA

1. **The Game: The Hidden Conductor**

2. **The Favorite Story / Comic / Hero**

3. **The Values**

4. **I Can Do That**

5. **The Ending Game -** demonstrate the chosen value using body language

THE GOAL of the workshop:
- to share the values that they cherish and respect.

MY FAVORITE STORY/ COMIC/ MOVIE HERO

1. **The Game: The Hidden Conductor**. The children are organized in an orchestra, and one of them is selected to be the conductor. The conductor makes different kinds of movements with his/her hands or head, and the orchestra is supposed to mirror those movements. One child plays the role of the detective, and has to find out who is the conductor. The detective gets out of the room, while the other children decide who the conductor is going to be. The conductor changes the movements when the detective does not pay attention, with the other children mimicking the movements simultaneously. The detective can guess three times, and if he/she does not manage to discover the conductor, somebody else takes the role of the detective and conductor, and the game is repeated.

2. **The Favorite Story / Comic / Hero**. The WL asks the children to say what their favorite story is or who their favorite hero is, and their reasons for choosing that particular story or character. **Sharing around the circle**.

3. **The Values**. From the list of values (Workshop 24), the children choose those that they have noticed in the character that they had chosen. **Sharing around the circle**.

4. **I Can Do That**. The WL asks the children to remember the situations in which they had proved such values in their own behavior. **Sharing around the circle**.

5. **The Ending Game**. The children should demonstrate the chosen value using body language. When a child demonstrates a value, the others mirror the gestures.

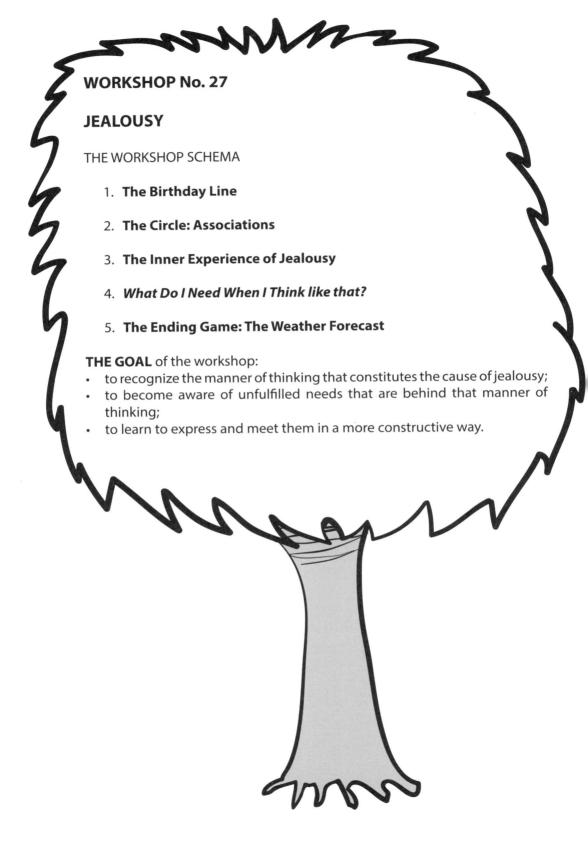

WORKSHOP No. 27

JEALOUSY

THE WORKSHOP SCHEMA

1. **The Birthday Line**

2. **The Circle: Associations**

3. **The Inner Experience of Jealousy**

4. *What Do I Need When I Think like that?*

5. **The Ending Game: The Weather Forecast**

THE GOAL of the workshop:
- to recognize the manner of thinking that constitutes the cause of jealousy;
- to become aware of unfulfilled needs that are behind that manner of thinking;
- to learn to express and meet them in a more constructive way.

JEALOUSY

1. **The Birthday Line**. The pupils are supposed to make a line according to their birth dates without any verbal communication. The WL helps by marking the beginning of the line (where those born in January should stand). After they have made the line, every child tells his/her birthday date. The sharing is about the feelings they had experienced while they were making the line.

2. **The Circle: Associations**. *Jealousy is when…*

3. **The Inner Experience of Jealousy**. *Where in your body do you feel jealousy? What would be the color of jealousy, if it had color?* They draw the body contour and mark where they feel jealousy and the way they experience this feeling and they write the thought that makes them feel jealous (i.e. "They prefer my brother to me", "She is prettier than I am") in comics balloons.
   Sharing around the circle. *Where do they feel jealousy? What does it look like? What thought induces jealousy?*

4. ***What Do I Need When I Think like that?*** The children are supposed to draw the comics balloon in the shape of a heart, next to the first one. In the heart shaped balloon they will write the need hidden in the thought that makes them feel jealous. For example, behind the thought "They prefer my brother to me!" the need "I need to know that I am loved as well" will appear in the heart balloon. "She is more beautiful than I am" will bring about "I want to believe that I am beautiful, as well."
   The children add this heart to their drawings and write their needs into in. Then they think how they can meet that need.
   Sharing around the circle. What is it that they want and how can they achieve it?

5. **The Ending Game: The Weather Forecast**. The children are sitting in a circle and they put their hands on the shoulders of the child sitting in front of them. The WL is sitting in the circle as well and starts making movements on the shoulders of the child in front of him/her, the child transmits them to the next child, and so on. The WL starts talking about the weather (for example, a sunny day, the beginning of a rain storm…) and, at the same time, makes the suitable movements with his fingers and hands on the back of the child standing in front of him. This is, actually, a great massage.

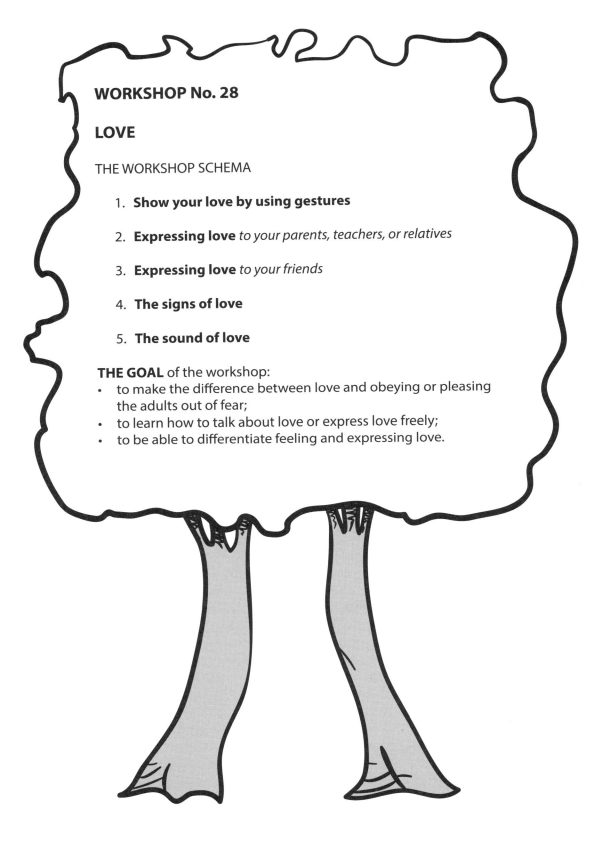

WORKSHOP No. 28

LOVE

THE WORKSHOP SCHEMA

1. **Show your love by using gestures**

2. **Expressing love** *to your parents, teachers, or relatives*

3. **Expressing love** *to your friends*

4. **The signs of love**

5. **The sound of love**

THE GOAL of the workshop:
- to make the difference between love and obeying or pleasing the adults out of fear;
- to learn how to talk about love or express love freely;
- to be able to differentiate feeling and expressing love.

LOVE

1. **Show your love by using gestures**: *Try to show love to the child on your right by making a gesture of love.*

2. **Expressing love:** *How do you show your love to your parents, teachers, or relatives?*
   Sharing around the circle: *Describe something special that you do in order to show your love to adults!* The children are free to choose the adult for whom they want to express their love: parent, teacher, or relative.
   The WL comment: *It is important that we should never mix love with obedience. We do things because we enjoy them ourselves.*

3. **Expressing love:** *How do you show love to your friends: to the boys and to the girls? Describe something special that you do in order to show love to your friends!* **Sharing around the circle.**

4. **The signs of love:** *How do you want your parents, teachers, relatives, friends, and boyfriends/girlfriends to show love to you?*
   Sharing around the circle: *Describe something special that you consider a sign of love that your parents, teachers, relatives, friends, and boyfriends/girlfriends made.* Children should be free to choose the person they want to talk about.

5. **The sound of love:** *show the neighbor on your left love by making a special sound.*

WORKSHOP No. 29

LOVE AND ME

THE WORKSHOP SCHEMA

1. **Personal space or distance**

2. **The game of associations: *Love is...***

3. ***How do you know when you have fallen in love?***

4. **The signs of love**

5. **Feeling LOVE**

6. **Ending game: Shower of warm messages of love**

THE GOAL of the workshop:
- to learn how to talk about love or express love freely;
- to be able to make the difference feeling and expressing love.

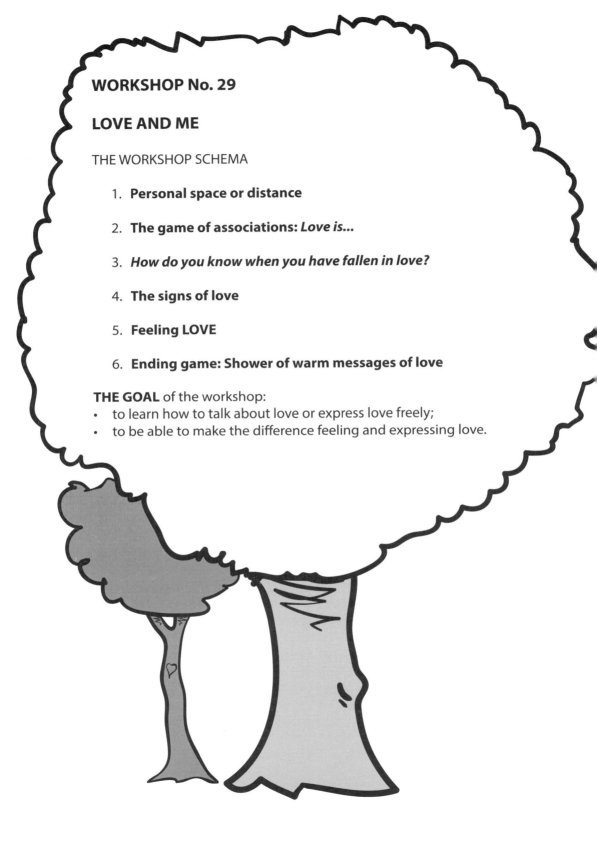

WORKSHOP No. 29

LOVE AND ME

1. **Personal space or distance.** The children stand in pairs, the boy and the girl facing each other, the distance between them about one meter. Looking into each other's eyes, they get as close as they feel comfortable. They stop when they feel the need to. The WL should pay special attention to the distance between the children in all pairs.

   When the WL gives a signal the children get so close to each other that their noses touch. Then they get as far from each other as they want.

   Sharing around the circle: How big was the distance between them in the first and in the third situation? How did they feel in each of the three positions? Do they recall holding each other's hands? Did they find it hard to look into each other's eyes?

2. **The game of associations: *Love is...***
   The opposite of love is...

3. ***How do you know when you have fallen in love?*** *What are the signs that make you aware of being in love?* **Sharing around the circle**.

4. **The signs of love**: *Do boys show love to the ones they have a crash on in a different way from the girls? Are there any signs of love that you particularly like? Are there any signs of love that you do not like?*
   Sharing around the circle: The children take turns in sharing about the way in which they express love for the boy/girl they have a crash on. They talk about the things they like or dislike.

5. **Feeling LOVE**: *What is the place in your body where you feel love? If love were colored, what would its color be?* The children draw a contour of the human body showing how they feel love, and marking the places where they feel it.
   Sharing around the circle: Where is it that the children feel love? What does it look like? They describe their drawings and make comments.

115

6. **Ending game: Shower of warm messages of love**. The children stand in two rows facing each other so as to form a corridor. A child at the end of the corridor passes through it as the children smile to him, tell him something nice and personal, or caress him/her. After passing he/she takes a place in the corridor and all the other children follow one by one.

WORKSHOP No. 30

EXPRESSING GRATITUDE

THE WORKSHOP SCHEMA

1. **The Magic Gift**

2. *Thank you for…*

3. **Making a Thank you Card**

4. **Sharing around the circle**

THE GOAL of the workshop:
- To learn how to express gratitude to people who did something that they liked.

WORKSHOP No. 30

EXPRESSING GRATITUDE

1. **The Magic Gift.** The children stand, arranged in a circle, and are supposed to give a magic gift to the person standing on their right. The first participant mimes an imaginary gift (i.e. blows a balloon, picks a flower, pulls a shell with a pearl from the sea, etc.) and offers it to the child standing to his/her right. The child that got the gift expresses gratitude, and mimes the second gift, intended for the next child, and so on. There is no verbal communication during the game. When everyone has got their gifts they check whether everyone guessed what the gift they got was.

2. ***Thank you for...*** The leader asks the children to remember some gesture of their parents, friends, siblings, cousins, or teachers that they liked very much because it was just what they needed at the time. Children are supposed to express their gratitude in three components. To state what it was that someone did, which of their needs was met, and how they felt at that moment. It is important that the children take notice of all three elements of the message: the action, the need, the feeling.
Sharing around the circle.

3. **Making a Thank you Card.** The children make a thank you card for the adult who made them happy. They write on it: "Thank you Card" followed by the name of the person they thank to, then they state what that person did, which of their needs was satisfied, and how they felt at that moment. The children decorate the card the way they like. They are encouraged to use different colors, lines, shapes according to their liking, and to choose the size of the card by themselves.

4. **Sharing around the circle**. The leader asks each child: "*What do you think, how will the recipient of the card feel when he/she gets it?*"
The last comment of the WL is that expressing gratitude makes all the participants in that act happy.

WORKSHOP No. 31

REVISION – A JOURNEY THROUGH THE WORKSHOPS

THE WORKSHOP SCHEMA

1. *How are you?* **Sharing around the circle.**

2. *Draw the "Line of the workshops".* **Sharing around the circle.**

3. *Play the role of objective evaluators of the workshop program*.

4. **Positive messages.** Exchanging positive messages.

5. **Around the circle game**. *Finish the sentence by making associations: When I am happy I would like to…*

WORKSHOP No. 31

REVISION – A JOURNEY
THROUGH THE WORKSHOPS

1. ***How are you?*** *How do you feel now that we have finished the program?* **Sharing around the circle.**

2. ***Draw the "Line of the workshops"***. *Try to draw a line so as to represent a journey: the starting point, emotional highlights, pleasant and unpleasant "stopovers", point of arrival, future destinations.*
   Sharing around the circle: *Give an account of your journey.* The children present their drawings and make comments.

3. ***Now, play the role of objective evaluators of the workshop program.*** *Write down the answer to the following questions:*
   a) *What was pleasant for you in the program as a whole?*
   b) *What was it that you did not like about it or bothered you?*
   c) *What was your favorite workshop?*
   d) *Is there anything that you missed and you would like to include in the program?*

4. **Positive messages:** *Write a personal positive message to each and every colleague in the group. Address him/her by his/her name.* (Each child should be given as many sheets of paper as members in the group.) *Do not forget to write the name of the child you write the message for on the other side of the paper so that you know whom to give it to.*
   Exchanging positive messages: One by one the children stand up and deliver their messages to each of the others.

5. **Around the circle game**. *Finish the sentence by making associations: When I am happy I would like to…(fly, etc.)*
   Give your own suggestion for ending. Children make a suggestion as to what they would like the ending game to be (make a gesture or sing something that the others are supposed to repeat, etc.)

WORKSHOP No. 32

PRESENTING THE RESULTS TO THE PARENTS

1. **The Movie.** The children try to make a movie, consisting of four scenes. The topic is "What have you learnt during this program and what was the most impressive thing for you?" It is supposed to be like watching four scenes from a movie. The children are divided into groups of 4-5. Each of the groups decides what kind of the story they will show (10 minutes to make a deal and rehearse roles). After that, the groups, one by one, enter "the stage". The presentation goes as follows: the WL tells the audience to keep their eyes closed, until he/she gives a sign. When the performers have prepared for the first scene, the leader calls "Open your eyes!" waits for a couple of seconds and says: " Close your eyes!" as the group arranges the second scene, and so on, until all of the four scenes are presented. In the end, the spectators (parents and children) guess what it was that they had seen. The performing group explains briefly what they intended to show. This continues until all of the groups have their turn.

2. **The Ending Game: Gentle Words**. The WL asks everyone to remember a favorite sentence said by someone to express tenderness or love (the parents should remember the sentence from their childhood), for example, "My sweet treasure" or "I love you the way you are". Everyone should remember something and keep it for himself/herself until the WL gives more instructions.

    Then the children sit in a circle, while the parents stand. They form an outer circle, so that each parent stands behind a child (if the number of people involved permits that). When the WL signals, each parent goes from child to child and whispers the chosen sentence (the same sentence to every child).

    The WL asks the children how they felt when they heard those sentences, whether they liked them. **Sharing in a group**.

    After that, the parents sit in a circle, and the children whisper into their ears the sentences they had chosen. The leader asks the parents how they felt while listening to these sentences, whether they liked them. **Sharing in a group.**

122

REVIEW

The 'Smile Keepers' program has been specifically developed for children and those adults who interact with children on a daily basis. It actively involves children in a series of stimulating activities, which promote changes in their lives.

The workshops are based on the interactionistic theory of psychic growth (e.g. theory where social interaction is the basic constructive agent of a child's development). These workshops effectively integrate techniques for relaxation, self-expression, and self-control building (based on biofeedback theory and various modern psychotherapies), as well as interactive techniques (derived from social interaction and social feedback theories). The essence of the program transmits through the sequence of the specifically designed interactive workshops. In other words, the main content and the main value of the program lies in the originality of the workshops (even though they were derived from biofeedback theory or social interaction theory) and in the originality of the whole composition of the workshops-sequence. In this very system the child is in the center of the program, and its psychologically stimulating activities. This way:

a) a child can 'open his/her heart' in a physically and emotionally relaxed atmosphere e.g. externalize inner experiences;

b) in the process of this externalization (verbal statements, drawings, scenes played out, etc.) the phenomena of catharsis and simple feedback, i.e. insight in what was externalized takes place;

c) externalization of individual experiences lead to the insight that similar experiences (e.g. fear, anger, etc.) do happen to others too, and generate insights concerning similarities and differences between other members of the social group;

d) children are asked to verbalize their own, as well as the experiences of others which helps them to learn about themselves; (e.g. to get explicit knowledge of what is going on inside of them);

e) in interactive workshops (i.e. those on sources of misunderstandings, social conflicts, nonverbal communication, etc.) social feedback is asked for, namely, how others respond to one's behavior and personal experiences, and there is a search for mutual solutions of mutual problems, so they can see themselves in relation to others and learn various psychological skills (techniques) for solving interpersonal problems, i.e. mutual constructions are developed;

f) Adults - workshop leaders have a discrete, but very important supportive role: to monitor the whole process of the children's development over the course of the workshop series: to discreetly organize workshop settings, to be special partners, all together assuring the success of the developmental process. In this system of workshops a child is an active participant, learning through experience, acquiring knowledge, techniques and skills, which will help to deal with difficult life events and coping problems. This experiential, educative system is especially beneficial in relation to the needs of children affected by war (refugees, children who suffered great losses, who experienced intensive fear or, more general: children under post-traumatic stress syndrome). And it should be pointed out that the program is also beneficial for children who live in our country today, where life is stressful in many aspects, because of the recent war, the destruction and poverty. In and of itself, the program would be a useful innovation in education, also in less dramatic, normal developmental environments, because of the active participation of the children, which is something that is to a large extent lacking in our educational system.

To realize all the intended and possible effects of the program it is necessary:
a) To educate workshop leaders in the workshop system;
b) to experientially determine the optimal number of children in each group; during the fist phase of realization;
c) to empirically monitor, if verbal instructions and requests are in tune with the developmental stages of the children;
d) while leading workshops: to feel at liberty to make changes in accordance with each individual group, the children's responses, and degree to which they are getting involved;
e) To evaluate at least the first effects of the program (do adults notice some changes in children who attended the program, how do children themselves view the benefits, are there any signs that the children apply some things from the program in the other contexts.
In closing, this program, and its many possibilities of application will hopefully attract a lot of support, because it is an important innovation in education, and could be really effective for children affected by war and for children in general.

Prof. Dr. Ivan Ivić
Developmental Psychology professor at Faculty of Philosophy in Belgrade
Belgrade, July 15th 1993.

A SHORT BIOGRAPHY OF NADA IGNJATOVIĆ-SAVIĆ

Born in 1947, **Nada Ignjatović-Savić** has been teaching and carrying out research in developmental psychology at the University of Belgrade for more than 30 years. She has conducted many research and intervention projects, and published several books and programs in the field of personal development, communication, social interaction and education.

Co-founder of the Center for non-violent communication "Smile Keepers", a non-governmental organization focusing primarily on human development, self and group awareness raising, reconstruction of educational practice and social change, Mrs. Nada Ignjatović-Savić was also its executive director.

From 1993 – 2001 she was the director of several intervention projects in education supported by UNICEF, EU, Norwegian People Aid, and Save the Children Trust. During this period she also offered different programs of education for peace and healing the wounds of the war with many groups from former Yugoslavia. During the period between 2000 - 2002 she was a member of the program committee and trainer in two international peace projects - "Olympic Games for Children" (participants were children and professionals from 10 countries) held in Delphi and Olympia, Greece, and "The Day After- Peace and Reconciliation Work with Israeli and Palestinian Religious Leaders, Business, University and Media People", held in Rome and Jerusalem.

Since 1993 when certified by Marshall Rosenberg as a trainer of Nonviolent Communication (NVC), she has been a co-trainer with him of many ten-day intensive international trainings, and has been very active in offering NVC trainings in European countries, Israel and India.

In 2003 in Pilion, Greece she taught NVC to the team of the project: "Human Rights and Conflict Management" organized by the European Network of Women, with the support of EU and Greek General Secretariat for Youth.

She is Coordinator for Serbia of the Earth Stewards Network, an international network of people dedicated to peace, global communication, conflict resolution, citizen diplomacy founded 1979 by the psychologist Danaan Parry. Since 1996 she is an accredited EP facilitator (Essential Peacemaking/ Women & Men). With Chris Gardner she offered EP training to many groups of men and women from different countries in Ex-Yugoslavia and Europe.

In the period 2001 – 2004 she was engaged by the Ministry of Education of Serbia and was a member of the team of experts assigned to develop democratization in education and reform of the school system. She is the author of the programs of Civic Education for Elementary School Children.

Nada Ignjatović-Savić passed away on July 19, 2011 in Belgrade.

SELECTED LIST OF PUBLICATIONS

• Ignjatović-Savić N., Kovač-Cerović T., Plut D., Pešikan A.: **Social Interaction and its developmental effects** in Valsiner J. (Ed): "Child Development within culturally structured environments", Ablex, 1988, 89-159;

• Ignjatović-Savić N.: **Le developpement de la cognition sociale chez les enfants prescolaires: une approche interactive**, in "Quelles recherches, quelles demarches pour que tous les enfants developpent leurs potentialites?", CRESAS-INRP, Paris, 1992;

• Ignjatović-Savić N.: **Expecting the unexpected; A view on child development from war affected social context,** in Psihologija, Journal of the Serbian Psychological Association, Vol.XXVIII, Special Issue 1995.

PROGRAMS AND MANUALS

• **"Smile keepers"** (two training programs for psychologists and teachers aiming to develop their personal and professional competence), 1993;

• 3 manuals **Smile keepers I, II, and III** - with programs for children aged 5-10, 11-15, and 15-18, published by the Institute of Psychology in Belgrade, 1994. The content of the programs is designed to help children to develop strategies to cope with emotional experience (fears, sadness, grief, anger), conflicts and to develop self and social awareness;

• "Mutual **education**", training program in nonviolent communication for professionals working with children, 1995;

• Co-author of the three manuals for teachers **"Words are windows or they are walls 1, 2 and 3"** offering nonviolent communication programs for children aged 5-10, 11-14, 15-18. Published by Institute of psychology, 1996. The manuals are translated to German, English, Polish, Danish and Italian, and used in many kindergartens and schools in Europe;

• **"Civic education 1 and 2 and 3"**- programs of civic education for the first, second and third grade of elementary school, published by the Ministry of education of Serbia, 2002-2004.

TABLE OF CONTENTS

OTHER BOOKS AVAILABLE IN ENGLISH:

Smile keepers I - program for promoting self and social awareness development psychological workshops for children 5 - 10 years of age. The content of the program is designed to help children to develop strategies to cope with emotional experience (fears, sadness, grief, anger), conflicts and to develop self and social awareness; contact: *book@krnvc.org*.

"SMILE KEEPERS" EDITIONS IN OTHER LANGUAGES:

• **Smile Keepers 1, 2 and 3** in Serbian (1993, 1995, 1997);
contact: *cncsmilekeepers@gmail.com*

• **Smile Keepers 1 and 2**

- in Polish (2009), under the title "Strażnicy uśmiechu 1 & 2"

- in German (volume1, 2015), under the title "Smile Keepers, Bd. 1: Hüter des Lächelns"; volume 2 to be published; contact: *www.synergia-verlag.ch*

- in Korean (2013); contact: *book@krnvc.org*

- in French (2017); contact: *sg@girasol.be*

- in English (2018); contact: *book@krnvc.org*

- in Chinese, to be published; contact: *book@krnvc.org*

CONTACT INFORMATION:

The Korean Center for Nonviolent Communication
3F. Namyang BLDG. 23, Samseong-ro 95-gil,
Gangnam-gu, Seoul, South Korea

e-mail: book@krnvc.org